WALKING ON AIR!
PARAGLIDING
FLIGHT

by DENNIS PAGEN

LEARNING TO FLY—FROM
GROUND ZERO TO THERMAL SOARING

ILLUSTRATIONS BY THE AUTHOR

WALKING ON AIR
PARAGLIDING FLIGHT

LEARNING TO FLY—FROM GROUND
ZERO TO THERMAL SOARING

First Printing: January, 1990
Printed in the United States of America
1 2 3 4 5 6 7 8 9 10 11 12 13 14

Published by Dennis Pagen
P.O. Box 101, Mingoville, PA 16856

Books by the Author

Hang Gliding Flying Skills
Flying Conditions
Hang Gliding Techniques
Powered Ultralight Training Course
Powered Ultralight Flying
Vol Libre! (French Edition)

ISBN 0-936310-09-X

ABOUT THE AUTHOR

Dennis Pagen has been writing about sport aviation—hang gliding and ultralights—since 1975. He has written eight books and over two hundred articles, all related to flying for fun. There doesn't seem to be an end to this activity, for as the sports continue to evolve, new techniques and experiences demand definition.

The author was raised in Port Huron, Michigan, and educated at Michigan State University where he majored in physics and electrical engineering. Upon graduation he decided to see more of the world than a tourist town and a bucolic college could offer. He moved to Boulder, Colorado for a year, then on to San Francisco, California, then to Leysin, Switzerland after touring Europe.

Dennis spent three years in Switzerland teaching skiing and mathematics at the Leysin American School. By 1972 he had seen enough of Swiss splendor and headed east. His overland route took him from Europe to Asia through all countries in between. After a year exploring the Orient as far south as Bali and as far north as Japan, he crossed the Pacific to the U.S. west coast.

In California in the fall of 1973 he witnessed personal flight for the very first time. This was hang gliding. After settling in Pennsylvania and buying a glider, Dennis learned to soar the endless Appalacian ridges and decided to devote himself to mankind's age-old dream of free flight.

Dennis researched and wrote his first book, *Flying Conditions*, in 1975. Also, this year he was appointed to the United States Hang Gliding Association Board of Directors and has served on this board to the present time. During this tenure, Dennis wrote the USHGA Instructor's Manual and helped develop many of the training and rating programs. His further activity in hang gliding consists of designing gliders, running meets as well as competing and teaching. Dennis has won numerous Regional Competitions and the 1978 National Championships.

Dennis first experimented with paragliders in Australia in January, 1988 with his first high flight occurring in the summer of 1989. He is struck by the simplicity and portability of paragliders and continues to explore this newest form of aviation with an interest in competition and leaping from mountains around the globe.

ACKNOWLEDGEMENT

I wish to thank Fred Stockwell for his invaluable aid in preparing this book. Fred spent days dictating the details that appear throughout this work. He also generously devoted many months of his time to the organization of paragliding in the United States.

I also wish to thank John Bouchard of Feral Corporation and Skip Beland of Morningside Recreation Park for their valuable input, but most importantly for their guidance during my first paragliding flights. Mark Chirico of Parapente, USA also deserves a word of thanks for he first introduced me to paragliding several years ago and sent along a stack of photos and information. Finally, I wish to thank Mark Axen and Marcus Salvenini for their contributions to the refinement of this material.

These and many other pilots helped in some way, great and small and I am in their debt.

Dennis Pagen
December, 1989

Cover Photo: Dennis Pagen
Photos in Text: Mark Chirico
              Fred Stockwell
              Claire Vassort

CONTENTS

PREFACE

Most everyone has had dreams of flying. Psychologists may impose heavy symbolism on such dreams, but how many psychologists leave their stuffy offices to stand on a windswept hill and watch a hawk soar silently aloft on gentle currents of air? We contend that the desire to fly is an end in itself and mankind has always had an urge to follow the birds into the sky.

In times past this urge was thwarted by the lack of flying machines, the lack of money or the lack of time. Not anymore. We now have a new method of taking to the air that combines the latest in technology with low cost and simplicity to bring the reality of flight to anyone willing to pursue their dreams. This is paragliding, the newest form of manned flight.

Paragliders are soft wings that look like colorful jellyfish floating through the air. They fly slowly, control, take off and land with ease and pack up or open in just minutes. They are so light-weight that you can put them on your back and hike to your takeoff point then be airborne with minimum fuss, away from the bustle of airports and traffic.

However, at the same time we mention the simplicity and joyful nature of paragliding, we must also point out the limitations of our sport. Paragliding is not like bicycling or skiing. It is a form of aviation with certain requirements that relate to safety.

We fly through an invisible fluid—the air—that must be understood in order to maintain control. Also, we must understand the behavior of our craft in different conditions and follow a few basic rules imposed by nature and man. All of these subjects are covered in detail in this book.

Once a pilot gains the understanding to master the beginning skills, he yearns to expand his horizons by flying higher and further. This book provides the careful guidance needed to take these additional steps in a careful, gradual manner. This book is not intended to substitute for an instructor, but rather enhance the teaching of a trained professional by providing drawings and details of all important subjects from first flight to soaring flight.

So with the emphasis firmly placed on having fun and flying safely, let's delay no longer. Turn the page and let the dream begin....

A modern paraglider takes off...

...and lands.

CHAPTER I

The Story of Paragliding

You are entering a new realm. This is a realm where dreams come true. For untold centuries in our dreams, in our poems, in our wildest imagination we have longed to float through the sky like a cloud, but when we returned to reality we were as earthbound as a stump. Indeed, non-dreamers among us would admonish: "If God meant for man to fly he would have given him wings." To this the visionaries would respond: "If God meant for man to stay on the ground, he would have given him roots!" Luckily, the visionaries persevered and now we can all float through the sky on personal, expressive wings. Paragliders. Welcome to the world of dreams.

This is also a world of unlimited fun with the possibility to expand your horizons beyond your present understanding. You will learn new ideas, and feel new sensations. Your viewpoint of the world we live in will be altered by your new perspective. Most of all you will find a way to enjoy a new side of living in the exhilarating domain of the sky.

By now, you probably don't need much convincing, but listen to the words of Leonardo Da Vinci:

"Why fly?
For once you have tested flight
You will walk the earth with your eyes turned skyward;
For there you have been,
And there you long to return."

With the latest addition to sport aviation—paragliding—we can prove these words true as Leonardo himself could not. We have at our disposal the most convenient, affordable and least difficult way to fly. A paraglider can be folded into a pack on our back, hiked to our takeoff site and readied to carry us aloft in minutes. We can purchase new equipment for a half to one fiftieth the cost of other sport aircraft. Finally we can become proficient at floating through the air in a paraglider after a few days of training rather than the weeks or months required with other forms of aviation.

One of the most attractive aspects of paragliding is the fact that licenses are not required by the federal government in the United States. This happy state of affairs will continue as long as pilots respect the airspace rules and fly safely. Our sport is self-regulating. It is the responsibility of each pilot to understand the few simple rules and fly accordingly. This book explains these rules in detail (see Chapter VII).

Flying safely is of utmost importance if we are going to continue to have fun with our new-found wings. At times the excitement and attention you garner in our sport may cloud your judgement. Consequently, in the course of your learning guided by your instructor and this manual, you will establish limits and strive to develop expert skills and impeccable judgement.

There are three factors that make up the flying situation: the equipment, the air conditions and the pilot, or as one wag put it, the *wing, the wind and the windividual.* We will look at each of these items in turn in later chapters. For now, be aware that you, the pilot will be ultimately responsible for all three items. The main goal of this book is to develop your judgement and skill while maintaining that necessary ingredient: fun.

So let's proceed with the first step of filling in some background on our sport then progressing to an understanding of our wings and the air. Soon you will be floating high above the countryside feeling like the bird you've always dreamed you were...

A BIT OF HISTORY

The development of paragliding was a slow process. As in most forms of aviation, it took a number of geniuses and dreamers who combined efforts and put together various ideas and experiences to bring the sport to its present state. The beginning was humble and as with most forms of aviation had military applications.

World War I was the stage for development of many technological weapons, including submarines. The only problem was, sophisticated electronics were not available to the sub drivers and their low riding profile made observation difficult. It's not easy to get somewhere if you don't know where you are. Enter the obvious solution: brave souls. The technique of towing a sailor and parachute aloft behind the sub was developed and proved to be a neat resolve of the observation problem. Unfortunately for the hapless sailor who we can only assume enjoyed his perch immensely, there were times when his vantage point impelled him to report a threatening enemy ship which resulted in the sub diving and the poor sailor floundering in the drink. The dread factor probably dampened the sailor's enthusiasm for flight.

After the first Great War, matters improved with the practice of land towing of standard round parachutes taking place in Germany and Holland. World War II put an end to such fun, but after this conflagration, there were over a thousand abandoned airbases in Europe and the U.S. These became ideal sights for parachute towing and the activity increased.

Things were far from ideal, however, for the round parachutes being used (see figure 1) created a lot of tow force to produce the required lift. Furthermore, they weren't all that controllable so release from the tow line was not highly rewarding.

Enter the Paracommander. This was a new style parachute with a more oblong shape (see figure 2) and cut-outs as well as longer panels and vents to propel the canopy forward in order to create more lift and allow excellent steering. This parachute was developed by Pioneer Parachute Corporation in the late 1950s and revolutionized sport parachute jumping as well as towing. The Paracommander would glide forward about 2.5 feet for every one foot of drop as opposed to falling almost vertically as did a conventional parachute.

The Paracommander allowed safer towing due to lesser speeds and tow forces required. Tourists soon found a new way to spend their Yankee dollars or pound sterling: taking rides high above the beaches of the pleasure capitals of the world under the gentle canopy of a Paracommander.

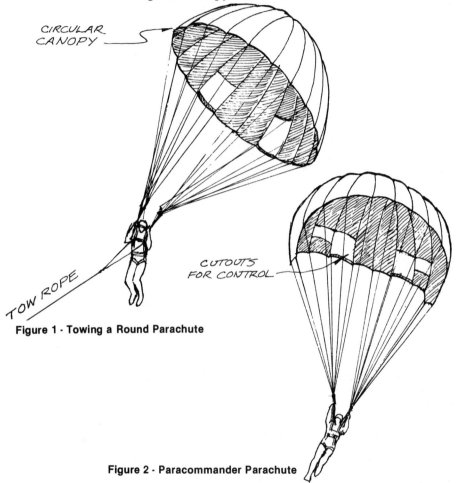

Figure 1 - Towing a Round Parachute

Figure 2 - Paracommander Parachute

The next evolutionary step was provided by the National Aeronautics and Space Administration (NASA). Their experimentation in rocket recovery devices led them to design various controllable parachutes including Rogallo wings which ultimately developed into hang gliders and ram air parachutes which again revolutionized sport parachuting and ultimately developed into paragliding.

Eventually towing ram air parachutes became the passion of a group who formed the British Association of Parascending (BAPC) in the early 1970s. They called their sport parascending, naturally, for the main event was towing aloft and staying aloft. However, the competitive spirit soon made its customary appearance and the passengers turned into pilots by releasing from the towline and floating back to earth to test their skills at spot landing.

The problem with these ram air parachutes or "squares" or "airfoils" (aerofoils in Britain) as they were called (see figure 3) was that they were relatively fast and unforgiving of poor landing techniques as a host of ankle injuries testified. The guest was on for better performance and more gentle characteristics.

Figure 3 · Square Parachute

In England, John Harbot and Andrew Crowley were occupied manufacturing square parachutes when they got wind of a few experimenters attempting to foot-launch the parachutes from a slope. It was soon realized that a larger size and different material would help (see Chapter II). This early experimentation led John Harbot to become one of the earliest test pilots, then manufacturers, then instructors in paragliding.

The name of the first person to successfully foot launch a paraglider has probably been lost in the shuffle of history. However, soon intrepid individuals were experimenting witth any slope they could find to satisfy their quest for airtime. By the mid-1980s the limits were found and a new sport was born: paragliding took flight.

PARAGLIDING TODAY

Today we know much more about training and techniques. The early pioneers had to find out the hard way what to do to stay out of trees and other unpleasantries. Now there are schools, and clubs to help you in your progression from admiring spectator to full-fledged pilot.

The only sensible way to discover the joys of simple flight is to get in touch with a reputable school and take lessons until you have mastered the minimum necessary skills—at least to the Novice rating of the American Paragliding Association (APA) rating system. The APA is the self regulating body of the sport on the North American continent and is a vital source of information concerning communication, instruction, ratings, clubs, and rules within our sport.

4

Paragliding has grown in Europe to be the most popular form of sport aviation. No doubt it will florish similarly in other parts of the world. Climbers have used paragliders to descend after arduous climbs up all the great peaks including Mt. Fuji in Japan and Mt. Everest in the Himalayas.

The possibilities open to a new paraglider pilot are many and varied. These include climbing and descent, soaring flight, tandem flying, photography, towing and competition. We will cover all of these items in later chapters, but for now let us continue to make progress in realizing our dream by preparing for our first lessons after a brief look at the future.

A pilot flies an older style glider.

THE FUTURE OF PARAGLIDING

No one can predict the eventual look of a sport so new such as ours. However, by taking a cue from other aviation sports—sailplaning, hang gliding, sky diving and ultralights to name a few—we can perhaps get a hint of the future. Without a doubt, performance of our canopies will increase. We will get more efficiency out of our airfoils and overall wings through various tricks of the designer's black art. Of course, this development must proceed carefully for the limits of design are as real as the limits of pilot skill.

Perhaps the key to progress will be the creation of better lifting canopies so we can stay up in lighter winds, which will enhance safety. Another approach is to use a more efficient yet smaller wing so that penetration speed is enhanced.

Other more immediate features are the use of thinner, wider canopies and the use of special harness seats that allow the pilot to shift his or her weight, pulling on the front or rear risers to directly change the canopies angle of attack. Both of these innovations have been experimented with and are standard features on more advanced designs. They are but an indication of the new wings that will eventually evolve.

Other practices bound to proliferate are the use of backpack engines to ascend with a paraglider in the flatlands and various forms of towing, some perhaps not even thought of yet. It should be clear that the sport will continue to develop as long as sanity and safety prevails.

The one possible fly in the ointment is the spectre of government regulation. If paraglider pilots are so foolish as to violate certain sacrosant areas of airspace or threaten the general public through unthinking behavior, we'll find ourselves with our wings clipped. We can prevent this simply by understanding the requirements of aviation in general and by banding together to both set our own guidelines and support each other in our search for freedom in the air.

PARAGLIDING AND YOU

You may well have some lingering doubts concerning the sport of paragliding. Is it dangerous? Are you in good enough shape? Do you have the "right stuff?" Legitimate questions to be sure.

The danger factor in most action sports has been exaggerated by the sensationalist press. The reality is that you are probably more likely to be seriously injured in your car on the way to go flying than you are actually flying . However, we aren't ignoring the fact that aviation in general is not forgiving of careless, reckless, foolish actions. The oft repeated adage, "paragliding is as safe as you want to make it," is an accurate statement, for the attitude of the pilot greatly determines the risk involved. You can fly with minimum danger if you so choose.

The physical requirements of our sport are not too great. The equipment weighs less than a golf bag and the energy output is less than an inning of softball. Sure, you may have to walk up a hill in training, but you can take your time. Really, if you can handle a few loping strides downhill and a walk off the landing field, then you can fly.

If almost anyone can fly, should they? The answer is no. There are certain individuals that are unable to maintain spatial orientation when they are moving in three dimensions (you probably know if this relates to you). Others have a confidence problem—too little or too much. An overly timid person may never have the will to step into the sky, while an overly bold individual may not listen to common sense. None of these individuals have a high probability of being a safe pilot and therefore should not enter the sport.

However for the vast majority, paragliding can be safe and rewarding. We invite you to put your doubts aside and join the "high" society that throngs to our colorful sport.

SUMMARY

The story of paragliding is still being written, for no story is over until the fat lady waddles into the wings. We do see a bright future, however, based on a past peppered with inspired experimenters and ardent adventurers. How can a future help but be bright when it consists of leaping into a crystal blue sky under brilliant canopies to waft away like a whimsical dandelion fluff? The opportunity is here for everyone to fly. There is no age, sex, race or creed limitations. Turn the page and begin the odyssey that will give your life a lift.

CHAPTER II

Your Flying Equipment

We have arrived at the first of the three factors that contribute to a safe flying system—the wing. Obtaining the proper equipment for your skill level and size is of utmost importance as is maintaining that equipment once it is under your care. Remember, in the air you are under *its* care, so don't neglect it and it won't let you down.

In this chapter we will cover most of what you need to know concerning your equipment, but be aware that materials, construction and design change from manufacturer to manufacturer and time to time. The ultimate source of information about your paraglider is the manufacturer that made it. Contact them directly or through your dealer if you have any questions concerning construction care or limitations.

Now with that caveat well in mind, we begin by giving names to what we want to talk about.

THE PARTS OF A PARAGLIDER

The entire apparatus that carries you through the air is properly termed a paraglider. This naturally becomes "glider" in common usage in order to save tongue energy. However, in most places in this book we will write out paraglider in order to avoid confusion with sailplanes and hang gliders, both of which are commonly known as gliders.

The colorful cloth that suspends us is known as the canopy or wing (see figure 4). There is an upper surface and a lower surface to this canopy as well as a leading edge and trailing edge as shown. The upper and lower surfaces are held together by ribs that are shaped to create a cross section like a bird's or airplane's wing. Holes or cross-ports in these ribs allow a spanwise (side to side) flow to equalize pressure and help maintain inflation of the canopy.

The ribs separate the canopy into cells. Each cell is defined by attachment lines along its sides, not necessarily the ribs. The cells in different designs may be divided into one, two, three or more chambers. The main reason for more divisions or ribs is to control the shape of the upper surface without adding additional lines.

At the outside edge of the canopy are stabilizers, flaps that are attached to lines for the purpose of keeping the canopy spread outwards and providing directional stability. On most modern designs these stabilizers are merely an extension of the wing which is pulled down by the suspension lines.

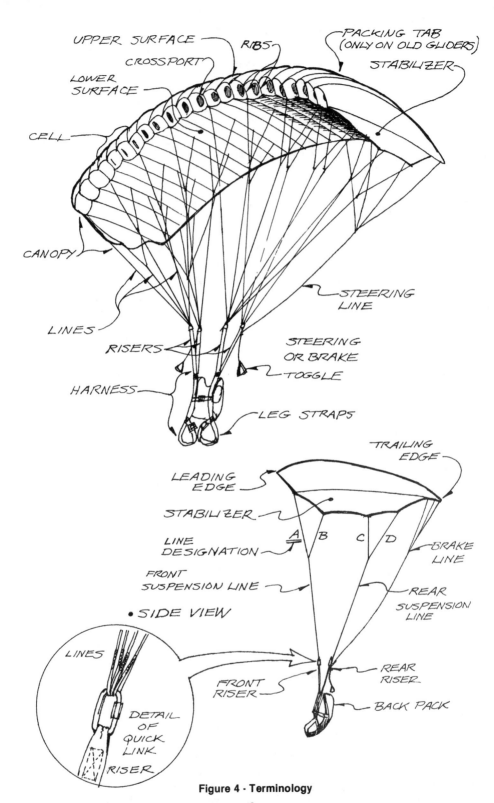

UPPER SURFACE

CROSSPORT

RIBS

PACKING TAB (ONLY ON OLD GLIDERS)

STABILIZER

LOWER SURFACE

CELL

CANOPY

LINES

RISERS

HARNESS

STEERING LINE

STEERING OR BRAKE

TOGGLE

LEG STRAPS

TRAILING EDGE

LEADING EDGE

STABILIZER

LINE DESIGNATION

A   B   C   D

BRAKE LINE

FRONT SUSPENSION LINE

REAR SUSPENSION LINE

• SIDE VIEW

LINES

DETAIL OF QUICK LINK

RISER

FRONT RISER

REAR RISER

BACK PACK

Figure 4 - Terminology

8

At the rear of the canopy toward the outside edges are the brakes as shown in the figure. The brakes are attached to separate lines, called steering or control lines, that extend through the harness and end in loops called toggles. The pilot holds the toggles to pull on the steering lines to thus activate the brakes for steering and slowing the canopy.

The support or suspension lines are ganged together front and rear. In most designs each line forms a Y at the top to attach in two or more places to the canopy. The lines in the front of the canopy attach to the front risers and the lines from the back of the canopy attach to the rear risers by means of a rapid or quick link. The suspension lines are designated A, B, C, and D lines from front to rear, respectively.

The harness itself consists of the risers as well as the seat and additional webbing for support and security. In most well-thought-out designs, the rear of the harness can carry the stowing bag or converts to a backpack that holds the entire canopy and rigging for a convenient way to stow and tote your wing after a pleasant day of flying.

PARAGLIDER CONSTRUCTION

The materials used in a paraglider are of high quality and have proven their worth in aviation and other sports over the years. Here is a brief look at what you'll be flying under to give you an idea of the importance of careful construction and maintenance.

Older canopies are sewn from non-porous coated Ripstop Nylon. Newer canopies utilize double coated (for ultraviolet radiation protection) Ripstop Dacron polyester which stretches less and can be much lighter in weight. Dacron canopies feel crisp and somewhat stiff as compared to Nylon canopies that feel soft like silk. The Dacron canopies are much easier to use since their lighter weight greatly facilitates inflation. A Dacron canopy is highly recommended over a Nylon one.

We wish to point out here that there is a major difference in canopies used for skydiving and paragliding. A parachute is designed to open at high velocities and is made of very porous Ripstop Nylon. This porosity is necessary to assure a lower opening shock on the skydiving canopy. Such a canopy would be much more difficult to foot launch. A paraglider canopy performs better and maintains inflation despite its smaller cell vents due to its lower porosity, but it would probably explode if it were ever deployed in a free-fall situation, for while it's plenty strong enough for our applications, it isn't meant to stop a plummeting person.

The thread used to sew a canopy is a parachute quality Nylon or Dacron and any repairs must match the material and size of the original. The suspension lines of a glider are made from Dacron, Kevlar or Spectra. Nylon must not be used here for it stretches much more than the former mentioned materials and line length stability is critical. We will see how to check these lines for proper length in Chapter V. Suspension lines should be rated for a minimum strength of 200 pounds (90 kg). Never replace these lines yourself—that is a manufacturer's job.

The suspension lines are routed to a stainless steel link at the harness that should be rated for no less than 900 pounds (410 kg). If you replace such a link with a hardware store item, be absolutely sure of its rated strength before you trust your life to its integrity. It is far better to get replacement links from a reputable dealer or direct from the manufacturer.

The steering lines are routed through rings or grommets on the rear risers. It is important that the toggle webbing or the knots that tie the toggles to the steering lines be constructed so as not to catch in the ring or grommet guide (see figure 5) or loss of controllability may result. Tie the line around the toggle itself.

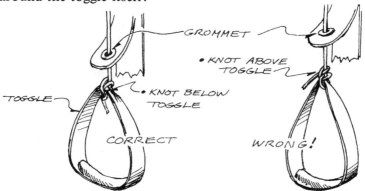

Figure 5 · Proper Toggle Attachment

This ensemble along with the harness makes up the paraglider as we know it today. The future may introduce new design permutations, but if we depart from the basic scheme we have here we will lose some of the attraction of paragliding, namely, simplicity and light weight. In fact, the average paraglider only weighs around ten pounds (4.5 kg). Some small descent models check in at less than half that weight. Not bad for a man-carrying aircraft.

THE HARNESS

Most harnesses are constructed of Dacron webbing and sewn with stout Dacron thread (type 3 should be a minimum standard). Harnesses should preferably have sewn joints in the form of a running W as shown in figure 6. A box stitch, (also shown) is a second best solution. The W system is stronger if some force tries to pull the webbing apart. Of course, all buckles and similar connectors must be made of parachute quality material and construction.

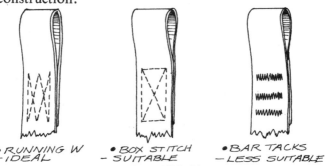

Figure 6 · Proper Stitching

There are several types of harnesses available to suit different needs. The simple sling harness is useful for training and for climbing/descent due to it's light weight. The drawbacks of this harness as shown in figure 7 is its fundamental lack of support. If you plan a long flight in such a basic harness, expect to walk like a chimpanzee for a while after you land.

The seat harness shown in figure 7 is more comfortable and is certainly recommended for soaring (sustained) flights. Its only drawback is its additional weight and possibly some restriction of running during launch.

The same can be said of the ultimate in harness comfort, the supine harness as shown in the figure. This arrangement lets you ease back in comfort while you arc through the sky. The legs, back and often head are supported for a truly relaxed flight. The laid-back position allows you to keep a watchful eye on the canopy—not a bad thing—but the unfamiliar flying position may be disconcerting to new pilots and should be used only after a number of hours of airtime are accummulated.

The fourth type of harness shown in figure 7 is the three riser harness. This harness allows the pilot to vary the angle of attack of the canopy directly by tilting forward and back, thus effectively shortening or lengthening lines. (A four riser harness is also available which works in essentially the same manner.) These harnesses usually are not used by

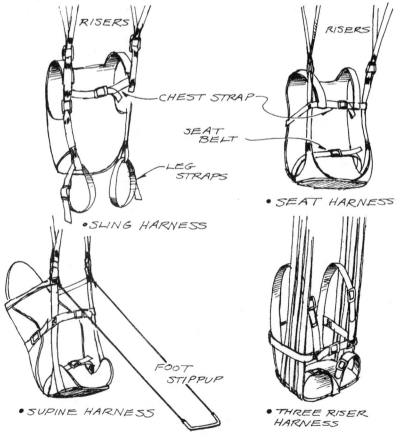

Figure 7 - Harness Types

beginners due to their additional control requirements. We will explore the use of three and four riser harnesses in Chapter VIII.

A DESIGN FOR BEGINNERS

Before you can soar like an eagle, you must learn to hop like a crow. It doesn't serve to have eagle wings when you're trying to do these crow hops either. For that reason your training school uses docile gliders that have a benign, forgiving personality. You should look for these features also when you purchase your first wing. A beginning glider is generally of low span (width) with more chord (front to rear distance) and large, open cells. The lesser span assures directional stability and reduces the chance of a cell closure. The large cells do the same. A further attribute of such a design is speeds slow enough to give an inexperienced pilot time to think and provide ease of takeoff and landing.

Again we recommend a canopy made of Dacron as the lighter weight material is much easier to inflate. This is an important matter for the beginner learning in light winds.

BUYING NEW EQUIPMENT

The two most important factors to consider when looking for a glider to purchase are its size and aspect ratio. The size of the canopy is important because a canopy too big will fly too slowly and may not inflate properly and be susceptible to winds. This can be very dangerous due to the possibility of canopy collapse. A canopy too small will be more difficult to launch and will provide fast flights and hot landings.

We use wing loading to determine canopy size. Wing loading is a measure of how much weight per area we put on our glider. It is normally measured in pounds per square foot. An ideal wing loading for a beginning pilot is around .4 to .5 pounds per square foot. Figure it this way: If you and your glider weigh 150 pounds, you divide 150 by .5 and arrive at 300 square feet of canopy.

Wing Loading Calculation
Wing Loading = $\dfrac{\text{Suspended Weight (pilot)} + \text{paraglider weight}}{\text{Canopy Area}}$
Note: Find canopy area from manufacturer's specifications or multiply width (span) times depth (chord or front to rear measurement)

Of course, wing loading will vary with the design, so again you should consult the manufacturer's recommendations. Typical wing loading range from .37 lbs/ft² to over .9 lbs/ft², the latter being reserved for expert pilots on high performance wings.

The concept of aspect ratio can be easily explained by stating that it is a measurement of how long and narrow our wings are. Figure 8 illustrates the difference in a low aspect ratio wing and a high aspect ratio wing. The low aspect ratio wing is more docile, but does not perform as well as the higher aspect ratio wing, providing all other factors remain the same.

Essentially, the high aspect ratio wing will reach out further on a glide (see Chapter III), but then, it is not as forgiving of pilot error.

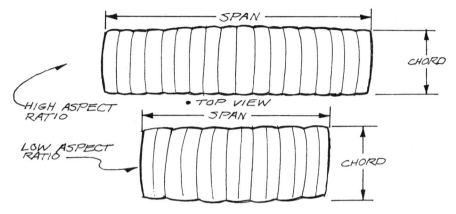

Figure 8 · Aspect Ratio

Generally, the aspect ratio of a canopy is related to the number of cells it contains. The more cells, the greater its span. Hence we generally ~~remove our earlier change~~ recommend a seven or nine cell glider for beginners while eleven cell canopies are for experts. However, some manufacturers change sizes by changing every cell proportionally which may result in a large seven cell canopy being wider than a small nine cell design. Thus, aspect ratio is the only true measure of a canopy's shape and suitability.

Aspect ratio is simply a measure of a canopy's width (span) *divided* by its depth (chord or front to rear distance as shown in figure 8). However, if a canopy is not of uniform chord, we can take advantage of the fact that the area must be the span times the average chord, so aspect ratio equals the span squared divided by the area.

Aspect Ratio Calculations	
Aspect Ratio (AR) = $\dfrac{\text{Span (b)}}{\text{Chord (c)}}$	b = span s = area
But Area (s) = Span (b) × Chord (c)	
So c = b/s	
Then AR = b^2/s	

The aspect ratio for a typical beginner's paraglider should be from 2.0 to 3.0, with the understanding that newer designs have managed to enhance stability and thus allow higher aspect ratios.

When selecting your new wings, remember that it must carry you aloft in all sorts of conditions within the limits of your experience. Don't be lured by glorious tales of performance and slick appearances. You want to form a love affair with your first glider, and to do that you need one you can trust and literally live with.

Read the manufacturer's promotional material and the owner's manual of any new glider you intend to buy. Check out its specification sheet, construction and possible certification. All new canopies should be certified to a standard to guarantee their airworthiness.

Talk to other pilots to get their opinion of the craft you intend to make your own. Remember, pilots are fairly chauvinistic about the gliders they personally own, but after enough poking around in the landing fields you can acquire some concensus as to what wings fly like a healthy angel and which ones are lead sleds. When all is said and done, there is no recommendation like the long-term record of reliability a glider earns when it is used as a standard entry level model by many schools over a period of years. Seek out these old reliables for your first glider if possible.

CARING FOR YOUR EQUIPMENT

Once you take the plunge and get your own flying gear, it is important that you care for it properly. This care means storing, cleaning and repairing.

To begin, you should always store your glider in a cool dry place. Mildew brought on by dampness can destroy Nylon and heat weakens both Nylon and Dacron. If your canopy gets wet, suspend it for air circulation if possible, or spread it on a clean surface to dry immediately. *Never* pack it away wet and *never* let it dry in the sun.

The sun's ultraviolet rays are the one thing that deteriorates your canopy, lines and harness the fastest. In fact, the life of a paraglider is largely determined by how long it is exposed to the sun providing it has not been physically molested. It should always be packed away or put in the shade when not in use.

Exposure to salt water deteriorates Nylon, so if you go for a dip in the drink, rinse your canopy, lines and harness thoroughly with fresh water and let it dry as per the instructions above. In no case should you use soap on your canopy as it will destroy the polyurethane coating that renders the material non-porous. If you must wash dirt from your canopy, use warm fresh water only. A jacuzzi bath works fine on a bedraggled canopy. One pioneer pilot has had a canopy for over twelve years without washing and claims it still looks new. Certainly a lot of care when laying out or packing your glider goes a long way to maintaining its pristine appearance.

Here's a handy guide to paraglider care:

> ### Paraglider Care
> - Store in a dry cool place.
> - Wash only with cold or warm fresh water.
> - If exposed to salt water, wash in fresh water immediately and dry thoroughly.
> - Allow air to circulate when drying and dry in shade only.
> - Exposure to sun shortens your glider's lifetime. Pack it when not in use.
> - Do not use soap, sprays or other cleaners on your canopy (a Dacron harness can handle a non-alkaline soap only).

When transporting your glider, keep it in its pack to protect it from moisture, fumes and dirt. Be sure not to set it near exhaust heat or in the direct sun shining through your car window. And by all means, don't use it for a cushion or seat around the campfire at the end of a glorious day's flying or you may not have many more due to a decrepit glider.

The maintenance required for your glider is essentially that outlined above, but here are a few additions: Once a year you should have your dealer or a competent pilot inspect all aspects of your glider for wear and deterioration. If you see a loose thread, *do not pull it*. It must be cut and sealed properly then restitched if necessary. Finally, inspect your line length periodically. The reason for this is that they can shrink if they get wet or stretch through use. Generally, they all shrink identically, but if they all didn't get soaked the same, who knows? Figure 9 illustrates how to accordian the canopy on its side to carefully compare all the lines. If any one (or several) line is out of order (not leaving the canopy at the same angle as the others) it must be replaced. At least one manufacturer recommends an annual replacement.

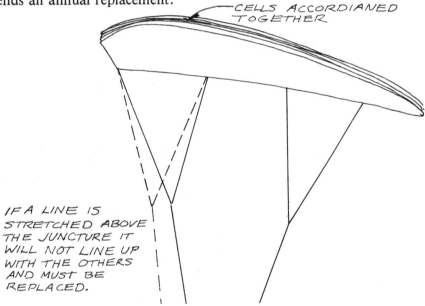

Figure 9 · Checking Lines

REPAIRING YOUR PARAGLIDER

Sometimes your wing will undergo wear and tear no matter how careful you are. The top surface can suffer abrasion when taking off in brushy areas and likewise the upper and lower surfaces when landing. Abrasions and tears should be carefully inspected to determine the extent of the damage and repaired as appropriate.

Here is what to look for: abrasions near the center of a cell can probably be ignored. Abrasions near the edges may have to be repaired if they are nearly through the material. All tears should be repaired with those near the edges more critical. However, tears near the attach point of a suspension line are not repairable by a general user and should be returned to the manufacturer or an experienced repair station for refurbishing.

The following guidelines apply to repairable tears: For small tears—less than 1 inch (2.5 cm) per side of the typical L shape—use Ripstop tape on both sides of the torn material. For layer tears, up to 2 inches (5 cm), use

15

patch material and a spray contact cement. Again, patch both sides of the canopy. Finally, for the largest tears, apply an appropriate patch and sew it down. Figure 10 illustrates these methods.

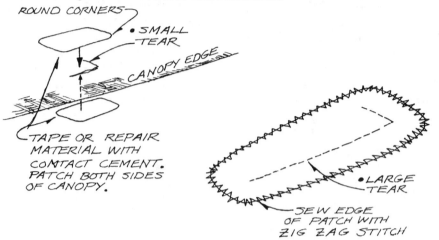

ROUND CORNERS

• SMALL TEAR

CANOPY EDGE

TAPE OR REPAIR MATERIAL WITH CONTACT CEMENT. PATCH BOTH SIDES OF CANOPY.

• LARGE TEAR

SEW EDGE OF PATCH WITH ZIG ZAG STITCH

Figure 10 · Canopy Repair

Other items you can repair are harness stitching and webbing replacement only if you have the correct strength material. Hand stitching is just as strong as machine stitching, if you take the time to do a careful job and use the proper stitch pattern and thread strength. You *cannot* repair a damaged line. It must be replaced by a competent dealer or the manufacturer.

Rapid links or quick links connecting lines will crack if over-tightened. On the other hand they can come undone if under-tightened. To avoid these ugly occurances, tighten them finger tight then add ¼ turn with pliers or a wrench. Do not allow these links to contact rocks or other hard items for scratches and hard blows can weaken them. Discard and replace them if their integrity is in question.

BUYING USED EQUIPMENT

Sometimes it makes economic sense to start out on used equipment, especially if you think you may want a higher performance model in a year or so. Expect to pay from $500 to $1500 for a used glider. As in any such transaction, the buyer must take care to get what he or she pays for.

It is best to buy a used paraglider from someone you know and trust. This may be a friend or a reputable dealer. If this is not possible, get an experienced pilot to help you look over the glider.

Try to determine why the seller is selling. Perhaps he is moving on to a higher performance model, or perhaps moving on to other things. Be sure to have him demonstrate a flight, and take one yourself if at all possible. If neither of you are capable of flying yet, try to get another qualified pilot to test-fly the gear. Perhaps he should be compensated for this service.

Now inspect the glider carefully. Look for damage to the canopy, abrasion on the lines, loose stitching on the harness and general appearance. Make sure type 3 thread (about 1/32 inch thick) is used for the harness and the buckles are intact. Be sure the glider is not homemade (there are some of those!) and make sure it is the right size for your weight.

Get down to brass tacks and carefully inspect the insides of the lines where they wear on the rapid links. Ditto for the inside of the risers. They may look pretty good outside, but sand and other debris can abrade them inside.

Finally, you must determine the amount of ultraviolet (UV) degradation. It helps if the pilot kept a log book, but the only reliable way to test canopy strength is a poke test. There is a standard tool with a specific radius point to perform this, but in the field you can use your stiffened finger. Better yet, have the seller perform the test by poking the canopy hard while you hold it stretched. That way if he pokes through he can't claim you damaged his canopy. If the canopy withstands this test you may wish to buy it.

Remember to do some pull tests on the lines, for they too deteriorate with UV. If any damage or weakness is detected at the very least you should consider the replacement of all lines in the price of the deal. As a final note try to buy a certified canopy but remember those sold prior to 1989 had no certification available.

TRIMMING YOUR WING

Sometimes general usage or abuse can throw your wing out of whack, so to speak. A slightly stretched canopy or factory tolerances may result in a glider that doesn't fly straight. To correct this problem, simply tighten the steering line on the side going forward or loosen the line on the side dropping back. You can change the line lengths by as much as four inches (10 cm) without compromising safety.

When making such adjustments, be sure to take frequent flights in smooth air to test your handiwork. Make each change a little at a time—about one inch (2.5 cm)—and then test fly the glider carefully.

Steering lines themselves can be stretched or perhaps misadjusted. The proper adjustment is found by letting go of the brakes with the canopy inflated. When the brake toggles are all the way up against the grommets or keepers, the brakes should just go off (no brake deflection of the canopy). If this is not the case, readjust your steering lines at the toggles to remedy the situation. Note that it is better to have steering lines that are too long rather than too short for long lines can be wrapped around your hand while lines that are too short will prevent you from achieving full speed, if necessary.

ADVANCED GLIDERS

Although you are far from the point where you should be considering advanced equipment, for the sake of completeness and future reference we will let you know what's in store and where the differences lie.

In general, advanced designs have higher aspect ratios with many more cells. Some designs have tails or elliptical planforms (projected area from above). These features make them fly better but also render them less stable.

Another trick to improve performance is bringing the upper surface leading edge forward and down as far as possible to increase the lifting potential. Some designs use a mesh in front to hold this more ideal shape yet provide inflation of the cells. Lower surface ports and completely closed cells are also incorporated sometimes. All these design factors improve performance but must be carefully applied or they lead to a dangerously unreliable canopy.

The final item we'll mention is a harness and riser system that actually lets you vary your angle of attack directly by shifting your weight to put more pull on the front risers or the rear risers as you will (the three riser harness pictured in figure 7). In this manner the pilot can control attitude, angle of attack and airspeed directly without resorting to brakes. The combination of this pitch control action and brakes increases the versatility of the paraglider considerably in terms of its available speeds.

However, such progress has its price. Besides demanding more cash, these gliders demand more expertise and attention on the part of the pilot. A standard glider flies at essentially the same angle of attack (see Chapter III) varied only by the brakes warping the canopy surfaces. With the additional freedom of movement presented by this harness system, more things can happen—both good and bad.

In Chapter VIII we discuss flying techniques on advanced equipment. Here we will simply reiterate that such higher performing gliders require more skill, more judgement and more attention then our fun beginning and intermediate models.

Advanced gliders soar Point of the Mountain, Utah.

ADDITIONAL GEAR

There are a few odds and ends that any complete pilot will want to obtain. Some of these are essential, like the helmet, and some are just for fun, like day-glo jumpsuits.

HELMETS—This piece of equipment is an absolute must, for any clumsy act can drop us on our noggin. Cheap helmets will not do. We recommend Bell type helmets with Z90 or D.O.T. approval. This means they will withstand a certain minimum crash force as well as resist puncture from a sharp object (a rock perhaps). Be sure to remove all visors, snaps, chin cups and protectors from your helmet, for they can snag lines and possibly leave you hanging uncomfortably.

EYE PROTECTION—This item can be very useful on long flights to prevent that ol' red eye—especially in winter—but the most important reason to wear eye protection is to keep your eyesight healthy if you go rolling in bushes during landing. Ski or motorcycle goggles work fine for our purposes.

GLOVES—Hand covering keeps your feelers feeling fine in winter, of course, but the best reason to wear gloves is to protect your hands from the abrasion of the toggles on long flights.

BOOTS—You'll see many pilots flying in sports shoes, but by far the best choice of footwear is a pair of ankle supporting paragliding boots. These should be available from your dealer. The next best thing are hiking style boots.

CLOTHING—It should not be necessary to say that adequate warm clothing is mandatory. Remember, mountain tops tend to be cooler than valleys and when you are out in the breeze there is the wind chill to contend with. A jumpsuit is a nice addition to your flying wardrobe and it has a practical side: it doesn't have as many loose ends to catch on lines. At the very least you should wear long pants - no shorts. Finally, knee pads are highly recommended in the early stages of flying.

RESERVE PARACHUTES

It may seem curious to speak of carrying a reserve parachute along when we are essentially under one. However, our canopies are designed to fly and any wing can get into trouble in strong turbulence. A reserve parachute can perform a rescue from as low as fifty feet (15 m) above the ground.

The ideal form of reserve chute is debatable, but here are the options: A side mounted, rear mounted or front mounted hand deployed chute, or a ballistic chute mounted with a projectile or rocket to pull it out. All of these systems have their strong suits and drawbacks and must be mounted, maintained and used as per the manufacturer's specifications.

Which ever system is used, the parachute must be thrown or blasted clear of the paraglider canopy. This requires a strong arm and a long enough parachute bridle. Of course, a longer bridle delays deployment, so a compromise must be made. No matter what system is used, it is sure that a second chance is better than none at all. We will discuss emergency parachute use in Chapter VIII.

INSTRUMENTS FOR PARAGLIDING

Various measuring devices come in handy up in the air and before we commit to aviation. Here are the important ones:

AIRSPEED INDICATOR/WINDMETER—This device, as its name applies measures our airspeed when it is with us in the air or the windspeed when we use it on the ground. There are several designs—little propellers or floating balls are the most common—but all work essentially the same way: the faster the air flows, the greater force it imparts to an object in the flow. Figure 11 shows a typical airspeed indicator with a tapered tube and a rising disc indicating velocity.

It is difficult to mount an airspeed indicator on a paraglider. Besides, with very little practice you can learn to judge your airspeed by sound and feel and thus free your eyes up for more important jobs such as avoiding traffic or large objects like the earth.

When using a windmeter, it is good to try to learn to judge the wind's speed by closing your eyes and feeling what the meter tells you. After time you can become a pretty good judge of conditions and resort to using your windmeter only as a cross check.

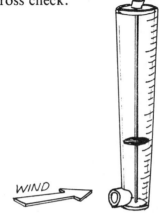

WIND

Figure 11 · Wind or Airspeed Indicator

Be aware that you don't always get a true reading of the wind's velocity at your takeoff point due to wind gradient, compression at the hill, shadow by the hill's edge or deflection. Gravity type windmeters only read true when held vertically, but then they are only set up to read a horizontal wind as can be seen in the figure. For this and other reasons you must develop your own sixth sense about the wind's strength.

ALTIMETER—This useful device takes advantage of the fact that as we rise higher air pressure drops. The altimeter measures this pressure drop and reports to the related altitude. You can find simple altimeters that report in 100 foot increments (30 m) or 1 foot increments (.3 m). The difference is largely reflected in the price. Electronic altimeters tend to be most sensitive and accurate thanks to their temperature compensating circuits (uncompensated altimeters may be as much as 3% off per 1000 feet). The more sensitive an altimeter is the more useful it can be, but the ultimate sensitivity isn't necessary for our sport, so save your money if you care and buy a sturdy model of medium sensitivity.

INCLINOMETER—Our craft glide down an incline—their natural glide path. It is very useful to be able to sight this path from takeoff to determine just where we are likely to end up. An inclinometer provides this opportunity by presenting a level and a sighting device to measure angles from this level. This is shown in figure 12 along with a device you can make yourself from a protractor and a weighted string. The first device costs more but works great. The protractor works fine but usually requires an assistant to help read the angles. If you mark glide ratios on the protractor ahead of time, matters are simplified (see Chapter III for a discussion of glide ratio). The figure provides the angle for various glide ratios.

VARIOMETER—A variometer or ''vario'' for short is a sensitive rate

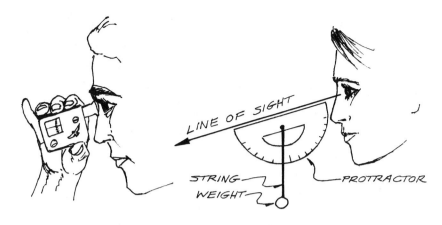

ANGLES RELATING TO GLIDE RATIOS:	
2.0 TO 1 = 27°	4.5 TO 1 = 12.5°
2.5 TO 1 = 22°	5.0 TO 1 = 11°
3.0 TO 1 = 18°	5.5 TO 1 = 10°
3.5 TO 1 = 16°	6.0 TO 1 = 9.5°
4.0 TO 1 = 14°	6.5 TO 1 = 8.7°

Figure 12 · Inclinometers

of climb instrument. It is very useful for soaring for it tells the pilot when lift or sink are encountered. As we shall see in Chapter VIII, mapping the ever-varying lift is a primary goal of a skillful soaring pilot.

Most varios are electronic and provide an audio and visual signal in the form of beeps for lift and a sick squeal for sink with a needle deflected up or down. These are very useful devices, but probably should not be used by beginning pilots due to their distracting nature.

All of these instruments can be purchased through your dealer or from shops specializing in other air sports. They will set you back a few or a lot of bucks, depending on what quality of instrument you opt for. Without a doubt all these instruments are quite useful and are fun little toys to help you enjoy your big toy.

SUMMARY ━━━━━━━━━━━━━━━━━━━━━━━━━━━━

In this chapter we have become acquainted with the material items that make up our great sport. This is hardware. We can touch it, feel it and control it. It is up to us to keep it in top shape and operating safely. That's not such a difficult job, for there are few moving parts in the traditional sense. But, of course, our entire flying machine is a moving part so our main concern is to keep it from moving into damaging objects. If we care for it, it carries us safely—it's as simple as that.

Next we will proceed to investigate some of the software, some of the intangibles of our sport. These items too are just as important as the hardware, so continue this learning adventure with our ultimate goal in sight: to fly with confidence over a rolling countryside, unfettered as the wind.

A pilot launches in the northwest US. Note seat harness and backpack.

A good flight begins with a good inflation.

CHAPTER III

Why It Flies

You may have gazed in awe as a jet arched high overhead, or eyed with wonder the graceful soaring of a hawk or even watched with envy as a paraglider floated high over the terrain, swooping down to settle the pilot back to earth, then gently collapse around him. The operation of such airborne entities may be a mystery to you but in fact, every flying object above a certain minimum size uses the same source of lift and obeys the same laws.

In this chapter we will look at a simple version of these laws in order to understand how our wings manage to carry us through the sky and how to avoid breaking these laws. We will learn some of the limits to operating a paraglider as well as gain a confidence in our craft. With just such an understanding we begin to work with nature rather than worry about unknowns. A knowledgeable pilot is a confident pilot and a confident pilot is on top of things—literally and figuratively!

THE AIR FORCE

We think of air as pretty light stuff, but a few experiences may indicate otherwise. Trying to ride a bicycle into a stiff wind or flying a kite on a breezy March day may give us an inkling of how forceful the air can be. Although all the weight of the air in one cubic foot—about the size of a large bucket—only weighs .076 pounds (.034 kg), in larger volumes the air's weight becomes significant. The air in a room 10x15x8 feet weighs over 91 pounds, while that in a house 20x40x8 feet weighs almost 490 pounds. When this much mass of air moves we feel the force as wind. Of course, when the wind is blowing, much more air than the volume of a house moves, and in reality, thousands of tons of air are moving when we feel a wind.

In light of this revelation, we gain respect for the air's punch. In truth, whether the air moves past us as wind or we move through it, the effects are the same: the mass of the air creates a force on a solid body as it moves past the body. Let's see why.

The mass of the air is caused by a collection of millions of air molecules, all of which have their own miniscule mass. Their inertia as they hit into us or as we move them out of the way is what causes the force we feel. This brings us to our first important rule:

What this means is that the force on our body or canopy increases greatly at higher windspeeds or airspeeds. In fact, if the wind doubles in speed, the force quadruples. An increase from a 5 mph to a 10 mph wind results in a four times greater force. A change from a 5 mph wind to 20 mph results in a force 16 times greater! Needless to say, as the wind gets stronger we need to be more alert and at some point flying becomes dangerous (see Chapters IV and V).

THE PENALTY OF DRAG

In this chapter we are most interested in how the air affects our flying apparatus. We should recognize right away that the air flowing by our canopy produces forces. If these forces are directed opposite to our flight path, we call them drag. Drag increases with the square of the velocity because as we increase airspeed (airspeed is the speed of our movement relative to the air, and this is identical to the speed of the air over our wing) we encounter twice as many air molecules per unit time and they are moving twice as fast.

In figure 13 we see various shapes in cross-section and the relative drag they produce. Note that some shapes have much less disrupting effect on the air than others. We call these shapes streamlined and they naturally ex-

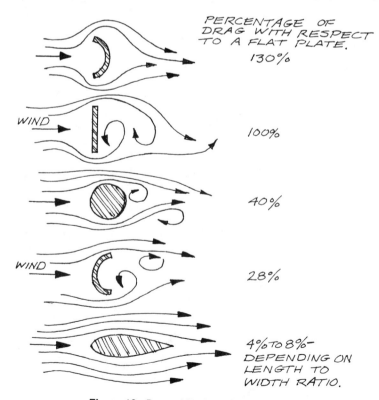

PERCENTAGE OF DRAG WITH RESPECT TO A FLAT PLATE.

130%

WIND

100%

40%

WIND

28%

4% TO 8% - DEPENDING ON LENGTH TO WIDTH RATIO.

Figure 13 · Drag of Various Shapes

24

perience less drag in a given wind. You may recognize some of these shapes as being used on airplanes or modern automobiles to reduce drag.

We have already mentioned that the velocity of the air moving by an object also affects the drag force it experiences. Other factors are its size and the air's density. The larger the object and the more dense the air, the greater the force felt. One reason why a canopy must be properly sized to the pilot is so he can handle the forces caused by the wind.

TYPES OF DRAG

It is helpful to our understanding to separate out the types of drag our flying apparatus creates. There are two main classifications: parasitic drag and induced drag. Parasitic drag can be further broken down into form drag and profile drag. The following chart should make matters clear:

TOTAL DRAG		
PARASITIC DRAG		INDUCED DRAG
FORM DRAG the drag caused by solid items exposed to the air such as the pilot and support lines.	PROFILE DRAG the drag caused by the skin friction of the airfoil (canopy) itself	the drag caused by the rearward directed forces on the airfoil that both lift, yet retard the wing (see figure 14)

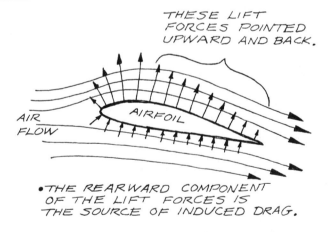

THESE LIFT FORCES POINTED UPWARD AND BACK.

AIR FLOW

AIRFOIL

•THE REARWARD COMPONENT OF THE LIFT FORCES IS THE SOURCE OF INDUCED DRAG.

Figure 14 · Induced Drag

Induced drag is the losses a wing undergoes as a penalty for producing lift. It expends itself by producing turbulence behind a wing, especially in the form of powerful organized swirls as pictured in figure 15. These swirls or vortices are always present and are one good reason not to fly closely behind another paraglider or aircraft.

To understand the cause of these vortices, try running your hand along the surface of water (your bathtub works fine). You will see swirls at your fingertips. These swirls are the result of the water escaping around to fill in behind your hand. In the same manner, air is being pushed forward and outward below your wing and escapes around the edges to the top. This constant flow creates the vortices as shown in the figure.

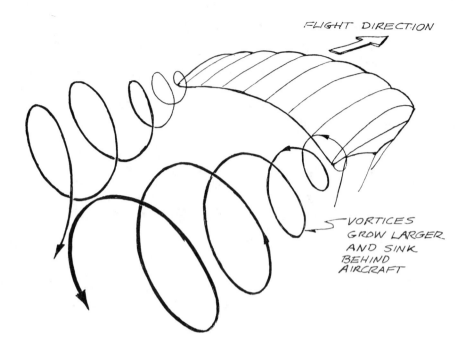

Figure 15 · Wingtip Vortices

THE REWARD OF LIFT

By convention, we call any force the air exerts on our wing in the opposite direction of our flight path drag. Also by convention (and for convenience), we call any force perpendicular to our flight path lift. In truth, lift and drag are but part of the overall force on a solid body moving in the air.

In figure 16 we see a cross-section of a shape we call an airfoil because it is an efficient producer of lift, while at the same time producing little drag. Note how it alters the flow of air around it.

In figure 14 we see the forces imparted on the airfoil by the air. It may be easy to understand the upward forces on the lower surface, but what about the upper surface forces? Here we see that as the air flows along the

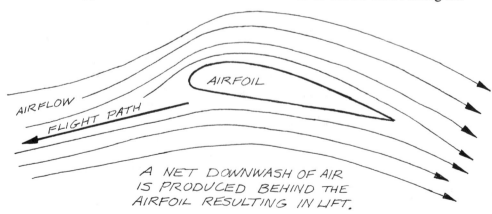

Figure 16 · Airfoil Shape

26

upper surface it must always shift its direction to flow more downward. As the airfoil imparts this downward movement to the air, the air imparts an upward force to the airfoil. As Sir Isaac Newton told us, for every action there's an equal and opposite reaction. About 2/3 of the total force is produced on the top surface of an airfoil and 1/3 on the bottom surface.

THE PARAGLIDER AIRFOIL

You may well wonder how a thin-surfaced flexible canopy such as a paraglider can act like an airplane wing. The first clue is to look at the paraglider airfoil. In figure 17 we see a cross-section of a canopy. The air entering the front opening inflates the canopy, with enough pressure to

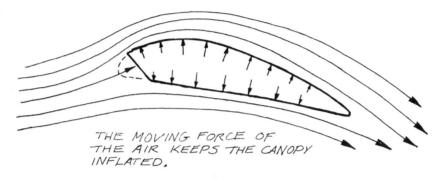

Figure 17 · Paraglider Airfoil · The Inflated Canopy

maintain its shape (as determined by the cut of the baffles) despite the lifting pressure from below. This shape is our familiar airfoil (without a nose or leading edge) which then produces lift and drag as with a conventional aircraft airfoil. As long as the canopy remains inflated we have a perfectly functioning wing.

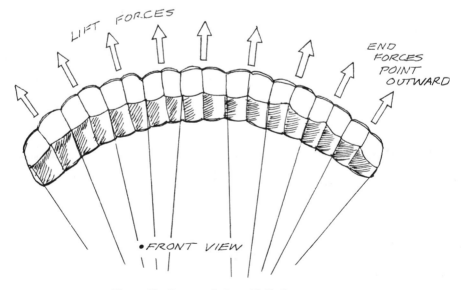

Figure 18 · Canopy Outward Inflation

27

Besides inflation of the airfoil, we must maintain the canopy from side to side. This is achieved by having a curved shape to the canopy when viewed head-on as shown in figure 18. Note that the upward forces towards the sides of the canopy are tilted somewhat outward so that they hold the canopy spread open against the inward pull of the support lines.

THE WING IN THE AIR

Now we can look at the sum of the forces on our flying airfoil. As we see in figure 19, we are flying along a descending path indicated by the arrow. The wind we feel is exactly opposite our flight path (always true in steady or equilibrium flight) as shown. The total forces acting on this airfoil are added together and appear as the arrow R. Note that R is exactly equal and opposite to the total weight of the system W. If this were not so, we would accelerate downward or slow until the forces on our wing build or diminish, reestablishing R exactly equal and opposite to W.

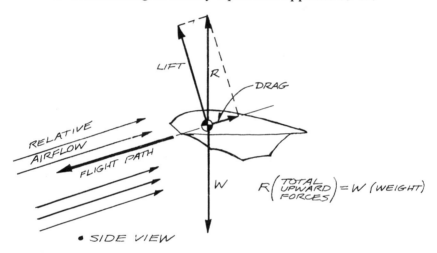

Figure 19 · Forces on a Wing

The upward force R can be separated into two forces for convenience. These are lift and drag. As noted before, we take as drag all the forces opposite our flight path while lift is all the forces perpendicular to this flight path. These are shown on the diagram. Note that the combined action of lift and drag equals R.

ANGLE OF ATTACK

We can understand a few more concepts by looking at figure 20. Here we see the leading edge of our airfoil (the furthest forward point) and the trailing edge (the rearmost point). The straight line between them is known as the chord and is really the measure of the airfoil's length. We also use the chord to measure various angles.

The first and most important angle is angle of attack. This angle is denoted by *a* on the diagram and is the angle between the chord and the relative wind (the wind the airfoil "sees"). As we shall see, all wings have a limited operating angle of attack range. Too low of an angle of attack results in a dive. Too high an angle of attack produces a stall which we'll hear more of later.

Fortunately, your trusty designer has set the proper angle of attack into your canopy by accurately adjusting the length of the support lines. Needless to say, they should not be altered. You can change your angle of attack somewhat, by pulling down on your front risers to lower the front of the canopy or pulling on rear risers or brakes to lower the rear. However, a paraglider has a limited range of usable angle of attack and these limits must be respected.

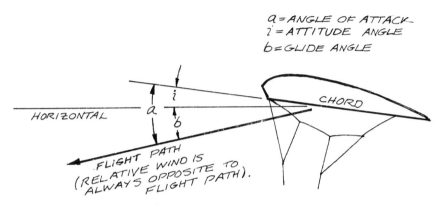

Figure 20 · Primary Flight Angles

ATTITUDE AND GLIDE ANGLE ────────────────

The final two angles shown in figure 20 are attitude angle and glide angle. The attitude angle is indicated by an *i* and is the angle the *chord* makes with the horizon (a level plane) as shown. The attitude angle is a measure of our wing's nose up or nose down position.

The glide angle (*b* on the diagram) is the angle our *flight path* makes with the horizontal. The greater *b* is, the steeper our glide path. This matter of glide path is important and will be dealt with later in this chapter.

UNDERSTANDING STALLS ────────────────

As an airfoil or wing moves through the air, or conversely, the air moves over the wing, the air must change direction as shown previously in figure 16 and 17. As we raise the nose or leading edge of our wing higher to achieve a greater angle of attack, we present more surface area to the relative wind and thus slow down. Both our forward velocity and vertical descent slows because we are deflecting the air more.

Since we want to descend more slowly to stay up longer, we may be tempted to raise our angle of attack higher and higher. But as already noted, there is a practical limit. That limit is dictated by how much change of direction we can force into the air flow. In figure 21a we see an airfoil deflecting the air at a very high angle of attack. The flow is fairly smooth and still "attached" to the upper surface. In 21b, we have added a small increment to the angle of attack and suddenly, the airflow can no longer bend like we want it to, it becomes detached from the upper surface and the wing is said to be stalled.

29

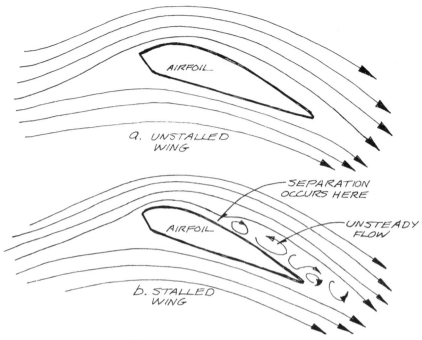

Figure 21 · Stalls on a Wing

When a wing stalls, drag builds up greatly as we can imagine by looking at all the large swirls we have created. This rapid build-up of drag quickly slows the wing so all normal flow and lift production ends.

The results of a stall are a reduction in control and a much more rapid descent. Needless to say, close to the ground this can be disasterous. In Chapter V we will learn how to detect, prevent and recover from stalls in detail. Here, let us just mention that avoiding flying too slowly (too high angle of attack) will prevent a stall in smooth air, and lowering the angle of attack to reattach the airflow and speed up is the recovery procedure.

Because the understanding and recognition of a stall is so important, we provide this summary:

Stall Awareness

•A stall occurs at one angle of attack only.

•For a given pilot this stall is one point airspeed in level flight, known as stall speed.

•A stall is caused by too high an angle of attack which is a result of pulling down on the rear risers or applying too much brake control.

•A stall results in loss of airspeed, loss of control, loss of altitude and possibly canopy collapse.

•Recover from a mild stall by lowering the angle of attack by reducing brakes smoothly to shoulder height.

CAUTION: see Chapter V for details of stall dangers and recovery.

Note that we said a stall occurs at a given angle of attack. However, for a given weight pilot, that angle of attack always occurs at one airspeed. Consequently we often speak of "stall airspeed" or simply "stall speed."

To put it simply here's a cardinal commandment for all beginning pilots:

THOU SHALT NOT STALL!

STABILITY BENEFITS

A primary quality desireable in any moving vehicle is stability. Imagine that if you took your hands off your car's steering wheel it went out of control rapidly. We'd have a lot of tracks across neighbors lawns and dented fenders galore. Stability of an automobile comes mainly from camber and castor in the front wheels. Stability is no less desirable in a paraglider and we shall explore its ways and means.

Before we begin we need some definitions. Firstly, stability refers to the tendency of a system (in our case our wing) to return to a previous condition (straight and level flight, for example) when disturbed by an outside force (turbulence perhaps or a short control input). In simple terms, a stable paraglider will return to normal flight after encountering a gust and will fly "hands-off" in smooth air.

To understand how stability works, let's separate the ways a paraglider (or any aircraft) can rotate. Figure 22 shows a typical canopy and the cardinal axes of rotation. Pitch is a change in angle of attack, nose up or

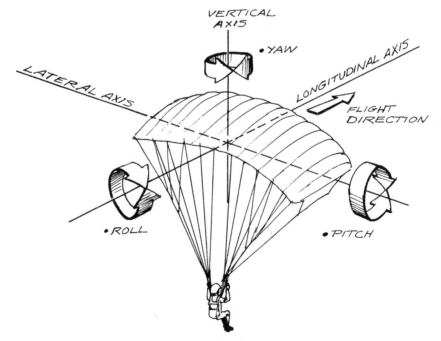

Figure 22 · Axes of Rotation

down, or rotation about a sideways (lateral) axis. Roll is moving one side up or down or rotation about an axis from front to rear in the center of the canopy (longitudinal axis). Yaw is one side of the wing moving forward or back or rotation about a vertical axis.

Now we can talk about the separate forms of stability. Pitch stability is derived mainly from the pendulum effect. Normally we hang directly below our canopy as shown in figure 23a. If for some reason our position is altered, by a gust retarding or accelerating our canopy, the balance of forces is offset as shown in figure 23b. Because our weight (W) is not acting directly below the upward forces (R), a couple or moment force is created to rotate the wing back to normal position, as in 23a. Pitch stability is the tendency for our wings to return to the pre-set angle of attack after being disturbed.

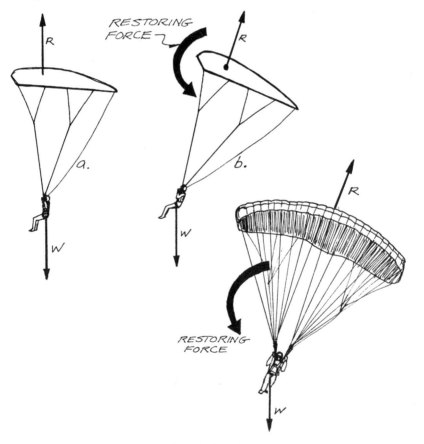

Figure 23 · Pitch and Roll Stability

Roll stability is really a result of the same pendulum effect. If our canopy is knocked to one side by an aggressive gust, the displaced forces R and W act together to rotate it back over our head as in figure 23c.

Yaw stability is a different matter. Some high performance canopies are swept or angled back at the leading edge so that if a yaw occurs, the side moving forward presents more surface to the air and thus drags back to equilibrium position. This action is shown in figure 24 and is the method of achieving yaw stability for flying wings such as a hang glider.

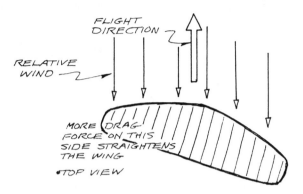

Figure 24 - Yaw Stability Due to Sweep

However, another factor is the most important for yaw stability in a paraglider. Looking at figure 25, we see the top view and front view of a canopy yawed to the wind direction. The shaded area of the canopy is the area behind the center of pressure (the point where the sum of the upward

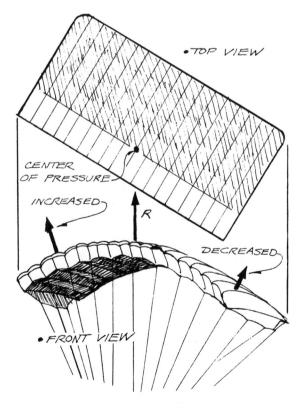

Figure 25 - Yaw Stability

forces **R** can be considered to act which is also directly above the center of gravity). In a yawed situation, the rearward displaced side of the canopy experiences a higher angle of attack while the forward side has a lower angle of attack as can be seen from the figure if you imagine your view as being that of the wind meeting the canopy. Now because the rearward portion is at a higher angle of attack, it creates more forces than the forward side and thus tends to straighten the canopy much like a fin on the rear of a boat or a conventional airplane. The trailing forces on the backward side couple with the force of gravity through the center of mass of the system to produce a correcting action.

All three forms of stability work together to create a wing that is safe, comfortable and easy to fly in a straight and level direction. However, we don't always want to fly perfectly straight.

TURNING FLIGHT

The other side of the stability coin is control. If a wing is too stable it will not react readily to the pilot's control inputs. Fortunately, a paraglider has a powerful aerodynamic control—the brakes—that makes it very controllable indeed.

We should spend a bit of time and look at how our soft wings turn. To begin, we initiate a turn by pulling on a control line. This pulls down the rearward portion of one side of our canopy, creating more drag and destroying lift on this side as shown in figure 26. As a result, the side of

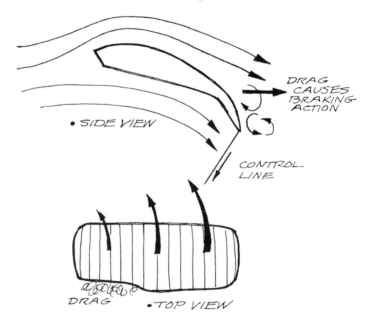

Figure 26 · Turn Controls

our canopy with the brake applied retards and drops slightly. Our body's inertia carries it away from the retarding canopy which thus tilts or banks the canopy. The forces on the flying system are then offset as shown in figure 27.

34

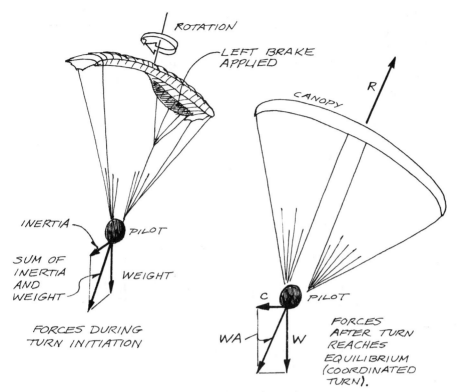

Figure 27 · Turn Forces

If the turn control is held, the canopy continues to bank, rotate and dive until our body begins swinging around the canopy much like a weight on a string. If the pilot holds the turn control at a given point, the canopy and pilot will continue in a coordinated turn at the chosen bank angle indefinitely. If he or she increases the turn control, the bank angle will steepen and a tight spiral or spinning turn will result. This can be dangerous and will be reviewed in Chapter VI.

Centrifugal force holds our body to the outside of the turn and is combined with our weight W to create a new apparent weight WA. This new weight is greater than W so R must be increased identically. This is accomplished because the added apparent weight (due to centrifugal force) actually increases our airspeed at any chosen angle of attack and thus increases the lift and drag created.

Because we are under the influence of centrifugal force in a coordinated turn, our body feels heavier to ourselves and our wing. This phenomena is known as G loading and is the same thing your feel at the bottom of the arc on a swing or rollercoaster. The amount of G loading varies with the bank angle of the turn and is shown in the graph in figure 28. From the graph we can see that a 45° turn increases our apparent weight 1.4 times so we are said to experience 1.4 Gs. We can likewise feel this increase in Gs if we rapidly pull out of a dive.

As we mentioned, the apparent increase in weight on the canopy pulls the canopy faster so that all speeds are increased. Our descent rate in-

35

creases in a turn as does our stall speed. The chart in figure 28 also indicates these increases. This information is useful for safety reasons as well as to understand performance factors.

Now we must not leave our pilot turning indefinitely. In order to come out of a turn he must simply release the brake control that is producing the turn (the control on the inside of the turn). At this point the natural stability of the wing will take over and the hapless pilot will roll out of the turn and commence to fly straight and level.

The following note is for pilots from other forms of aviation: In a paraglider, due to its extreme roll stability, you must continuously hold a roll control to perform a continuous turn. The amount of control you hold determines the bank angle. The control is not released once the bank angle is established as it is in other aircraft or the paraglider will unbank (this applies to both brake and seat controlled turns).

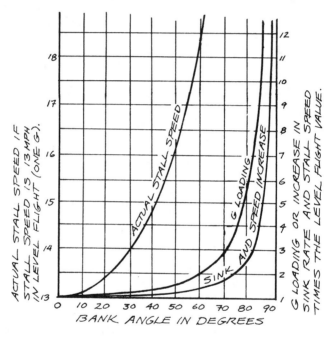

Figure 28 · Changes in a Turn

OUR BEST PERFORMANCE _____

When we speak of performance we can be referring to many things including handling, glide ratio, sink rate and speed. We covered handling somewhat in the previous section. Let's look at the other ideas.

Glide ratio is directly related to glide path because it is a measure of how far forward we travel for every unit of vertical descent. Typical glide ratios for a paraglider are between 3 to 1 and 6 to 1. This means we travel between three feet forward for every foot of descent and six feet forward for every foot of descent depending on the design.

Figure 29 shows various glide ratios and a representation of a canopy following a 4 to 1 glide path. Note that because lift is the sum of forces

36

perpendicular to our flight path and drag is always parallel to the path, the angle *b* (glide path angle) is the same as the angle between the lift arrow and R. Consequently, the triangle made by the lift and drag arrows and R is similar (the same shape) as the triangle made by Vh, Vv and the glide path. But Vh and Vv are the horizontal and vertical velocities respectively. Consequently, our glide ratio is simply Vh divided by Vv (Vh/Vv). Furthermore, since the triangles are similar we can set Vh/Vv equal to lift (L) divided by drag (D), so Vh/Vv = L/D. We often use the phrases L over D and glide ratio interchangeably as a measure of how far we travel forward as we drop.

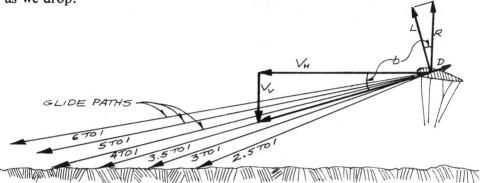

Figure 29 · Glide Ratio

The perceptive reader will perhaps note that if we can reduce the drag while at the same time maintaining the same lift our glide ratio will increase. This is exactly the case and is the reason some canopy designs perform better than others. The two main things that determine the maximum glide ratio (L/D max) a wing may achieve are the shape of the airfoil and the aspect ratio (see Chapter II).

Our sink rate is the speed at which we descend. For various reasons we wish to minimize this rate, not the least of which is to remain aloft as long as possible. In general, our minimum sink rate occurs when we are flying quite slowly (a wee bit faster than stall). The minimum sink rate of which a canopy is capable is mainly a function of the airfoil shape or "camber" of the upper surface and the size of the canopy in relation to the pilot weight (wing loading as discussed in Chapter II).

The camber of a wing or airfoil is the curve of the upper surface (in some airfoils the lower surface also has camber). In a paraglider we can increase this camber by applying our brakes. This works much like the flaps of a conventional airplane to slow our forward and vertical speed, the latter being our sink rate.

In figure 30 we see the relations between flying at our minimum sink rate angle of attack and best glide ratio angle of attack. When we are flying "best glide," we descend faster than when flying at min. sink," but we reach further out. Our glide ratio is maximized in the former and our descent rate is slowest in the latter.

Here is a handy chart to understand our cardinal speeds (Note: this chart only applies to a two-riser system. Three-riser systems are discussed in Chapter VIII):

> **Cardinal Speeds**
> •Stall speed occurs 11 to 14 mph (17 to 23 km/h) and is achieved by applying more than full brakes (about 3 to 6 inches more).
> •Minimum sink speed occurs with 50% brakes applied and is between 13 and 17 mph (20-27 km/h)
> •Best glide speed is achieved by applying 25% brakes and is between 15 and 19 mph (25-30 km/h).
> •Maximum speed occurs at 17 to 25 mph (27 to 40 km/h) with zero brakes applied.

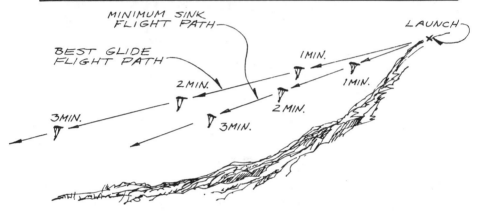

Figure 30 · Relation of Best Glide and Minimum Sink Flight Paths

The reason we can't be more definite about the cardinal airspeed is because wing loading (the weight of the pilot on a given canopy) changes these speeds, with the heavier pilot creating the greater speeds. At the forward speeds we are dealing with, we add about ½ mph for every ten pounds of additional weight (.8 km/h for every five kg added).

Our sink rate is also increased as we add weight. This works out to be an addition of ten to twenty feet per minute for every ten pounds added (.05 to .10 m/s for each additional five kg). However, our maximum glide ratio remains unchanged. This startling fact is due to the proportional increase of both lift and drag as we add weight so that the lift to drag ratio (L/D) remains the same. (This statement remains true as long as additional weight doesn't greatly change the canopy shape).

In this context we can mention the effects of air density changes. Thinner air acts just as if we added more weight to our wing. All the speeds become greater but our glide ratio remains the same. If we get 4 to 1 in Death Valley, we get 4 to 1 on Mt. Everest assuming no wind, of course. As we shall see in Chapter IV, various things affect air density including temperature, humidity, altitude and pressure systems.

GLIDING IN WIND
We spoke of achieving our best glide above with the assumption that we

were traveling in still air. However, this is a careless assumption for the air is rarely still. Imagine flying at your best glide airspeed into a headwind of an equal speed. You may be achieving your best glide with respect to the air, but you are no longer going forward and are, in fact, descending straight down. Not exactly a great glide!

Figure 31a illustrates the above and 31b indicates how flying *faster* than your best glide speed in a head wind actually achieves more distance over the ground and thus a better glide ratio with respect to the ground which is the important matter.

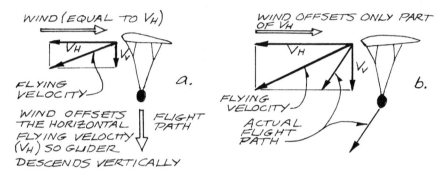

Figure 31 · Flying in a Headwind

In figure 32 we see how various headwinds and tailwinds affect our glide ratio over the ground. In no manner can we expect to get a better glide ratio than our still air glide ratio in a headwind. With a tailwind however, we're given a boost with added velocity over the ground as we sink at the same rate. Thus, we achieve a better glide in a tailwind.

To understand more about this matter, let's graph a paraglider's performance.

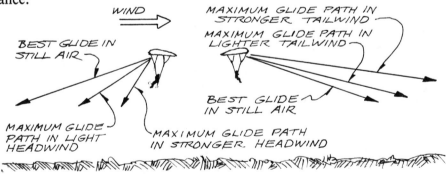

Figure 32 · Glide in Various Winds

THE PERFORMANCE MAP

If we could measure our horizontal velocity and our vertical velocity at every angle of attack or brake setting we would have a graph looking much like that of figure 33. (Note that technically speaking applying brakes changes the angle of attack of our wings since the trailing edge is brought downward. However, we aren't changing angle of attack in the traditional sense unless we pull down the front or rear risers. Consequently, our graph is not as flat as those plotted for other types of aircraft.) We call this graph a performance map or polar.

We can see several things on our polar. For example, the highest point on the polar gives us our minimum sink rate and is about 500 feet per minute in the example (point A). This point occurs at a horizontal speed of around 17 mph.

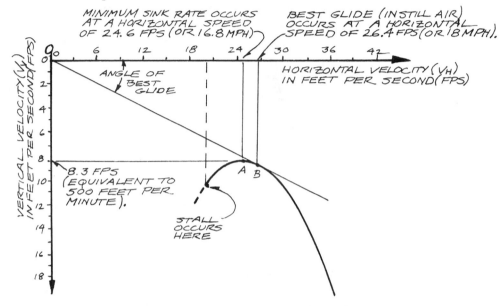

Figure 33 · A Typical Glider's Polar or Performance Map

Next we can take any point on the graph and find its corresponding horizontal and vertical velocity (Vh and Vv). If we know these values, we can find the glide ratio at each point for Vh/Vv is the glide ratio. Armed with this knowledge we can then proceed to find our maximum glide ratio by drawing a tangent line from the origin O to the curve (line OB). The reason this line represents our maximum glide ratio is because a line to any other point on the curve other than the tangent point B will have a steeper slope than the line OB. The point B is in fact our best glide point. Moving straight up to our horizontal velocity line, we see that this best glide occurs at 18 mph.

Before we leave this nice graph, we can see two more things. First, increasing our wing loading simply moves the curve along the best glide line as shown in figure 34. Best glide remains the same while all speeds (including sink rates) increase.

Secondly, we see what to do in a headwind. A wind has the affect of moving the curve left or right. But instead of moving the curve, we can move the origin. For example, assume we have a 10 mph headwind. We simply move to the right of the origin an amount equal to 10 mph and place our new origin O'. Then we draw our tangent line to the curve and arrive at D. Line O'D is our tangent line describing our best glide ratio in a

10 mph headwind. Our speed to achieve this becomes 19.2 mph which is, of course, faster than the best glide speed in still air (18 mph). We can likewise move the axis origin left for a tailwind, up for sink or down for lift to find the optimum glide path speed.

The performance of a paraglider is fairly limited to what the manufacturer designs into the canopy. We as pilots cannot vary it too much in flight. However, it behooves us to understand how to alter our performance as much as possible to maximize our potential fun and safety in all situations.

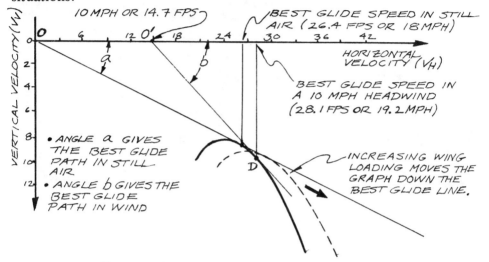

Figure 34 · Wing Loading and Wind Effects on the Polar

SUMMARY

The subject of aerodynamics in general and the mechanisms of paraglider flight in particular is as fascinating as it can be demanding. It can also be a life-long pursuit. We have endeavored here to present the highlights and important ideas relating to how our wings work in the air. The purpose for this is to instill confidence in the pilot as well as the ability to recognize and solve problems. As you continue with your experience in this great sport you will gain familiarity with some of the terms and ideas and can absorb more of this technical information.

At the very least, we should understand the concepts of lift and drag, angle of attack and stall. The difference between minimum sink and best glide ratio is also important for maximizing performance and keeping us out of trouble.

Take a breather and think about the ideas we have presented, then reread the material after you've had some practical experience. You'll find the concepts come easier and you will begin to fully appreciate the ingenious device that lets you walk on air.

An instructor pushes a pilot in higher winds. Note the three riser harness.

The author flying in a steering seat.

CHAPTER IV

Understanding the Restless Air

Now we have arrived at the second factor that makes up our safe flying trio—the wind. You have spent all your life feeling the wind in its different guises, from the warm gentle breezes of summer to the artic gusts of deep winter. But perhaps you didn't really think about the causes of such wind variation or what concern this is to a creature of the air.

You are now unraveling your cocoon to become such a creature. And yes, you must learn the ways of the wind for you will soon have an intimate relationship with the sky. We fly for pure joy, but joy can turn to stark terror if we get caught in powerful conditions beyond our understanding. For this reason every safe and sane pilot learns all he or she can about weather conditions through observation, reading and word of mouth. This learning is fun, for your knowledge is put to instant use as you take a flight and feel the texture and measure of the wind.

In this chapter we will explore the knowledge necessary to make you a competent and safe pilot. Later in Chapter VIII we delve deeper into the mysteries of the air to look at further complications and soaring possibilities. Of course, acquiring a birdlike understanding of the air is a lifelong pursuit and even a basic course is beyond the scope of this manual. For that reason we direct you to our companion book, *Flying Conditions*. This book provides you with all the details you need to fully comprehend the ways of the sky. *Flying Conditions* is available from your paragliding dealer, in other sport aviation shops or from the publisher (see the address at the front of this book).

AIR—THE SLIPPERY FLUID

We begin our exploration of the air by finding out what it is. Air is a gas made up of molecules that easily slide by one another and allow a solid to move through without giving much resistance, at least at slow speeds. The molecular content of the air is 99% nitrogen and oxygen with some carbon dioxide and other pollutants added through natural causes or mankind's excesses.

One other important constituent of air is water vapor. Water evaporates and turns to a gas to mix with the air, but also condenses back to water when the air is sufficiently cooled. During this evaporation and condensation process, great heat is exchanged with the atmosphere, which has a significance we'll look at in Chapter VIII. For now, we'll be content to know that the water vapor present in the air varies from time to time according to the availability of water near the air (lakes, humid ground or living greenery) and the air temperature (warmer air can hold more water vapor). The main effect this has on our flying is that the more humid the air is (the more water vapor it contains), the less dense it is. This may seem strange at first if we are accustomed to think of water as a weighty liquid, but the fact is, water molecules are lighter than oxygen or nitrogen molecules and so evaporated water lightens the air.

The density of the air is an important factor determining how our wings fly as we discovered in Chapter III. Besides water vapor content, the temperature of the air and our height above the ground serves to vary the air density we encounter. Warmer air is less dense than cooler air. You might have the impression that heating the air gives it more energy, which is true, but in an open system like the atmosphere, as the air is heated it spreads out and thus becomes less dense.

If we vary our position up or down, we experience less or greater air density. This is because the air itself has weight. Gravity pulls it downward so the lower a molecule is the more of its buddies it has to hold up. The poor chaps at the bottom are squeezed together while the happy fellows at the top of the heap go zipping around without much weight on them at all. The residents in the upper levels of the atmosphere are under much less pressure than those below and are thus less densely packed. In fact, although the atmosphere (gaseous shroud around the earth) extends upwards of 500 miles (800 km), over half of its total weight is below 18,000 feet (5,500 m)!

The density of the air does not vary in a simple manner with altitude. However, in the lower 10,000 feet (3,000 m) the relationship can be considered linear and is about a 3% drop per 1000 ft (305m) gain in altitude. It has been this author's personal experience that in inflating a canopy on level ground in no wind at 9,000 ft is a difficult task indeed due to the lower density.

We summarize all the material in this section in the table below:

Air Density Changes
Air density goes down as:
1. Humidity increases
2. Temperature rises
3. Altitude increases.

Important Safety Tip
We must understand that since all speeds increase with lower density, trying to take off on a hot, humid day at a high altitude site may require a bit of wind to assist us or we may be just spinning our wheels. Conversely, on cold winter days at low altitudes, the air is more dense so our upper wind limit should be lower.

THE CIRCULATING AIR

Now that we know a little about the air's structure, let's see how it moves and changes. If you live in the temperate areas of North America or Europe, you are familiar with the changeable nature of the weather. In fact, in these areas, the only constant thing about the weather is that it will change.

Tropical areas display weather that changes much more slowly—usually a season of sun and a season of rain. The reason for these differences is the overall circulations of the atmosphere. The engine for this circulation is the sun.

The sun heats the equator much more readily than the pole areas of the earth. This causes rising air currents in the equatorial areas (remember, warmer air is less dense and therefore rises to its equilibrium level). These currents head north towards the poles, but don't make it. They are tripped up by the Coriolis effect which is a result of the earth turning below the moving air. As a consequence, the northward moving upper air turns right and piles up around 30° latitude. This "piling up" of air in the upper atmosphere results in more pressure on the surface and we have a band of high pressure around the earth near 30° latitude. This high pressure band is the force behind our warm winds that come from the south (see figure 35).

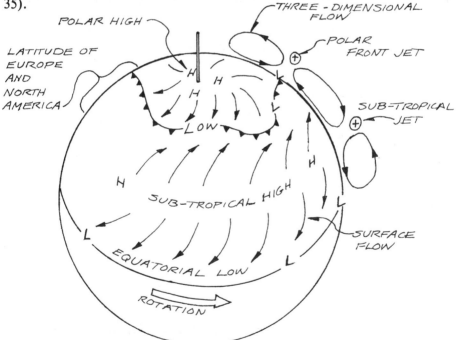

Figure 35 · Circulation on the Earth

Meanwhile, some of the air continues northward in the upper atmosphere to pile up at the north pole. This air becomes cold and dense, creating another band of high pressure systems in the north. These highs push cold air southward. We can see then that there is a conflict of warm

45

air meeting cold air in the temperate zones. We are in a battle zone and sometimes the victor is the southern, warm air mass, sometimes the northern mass. The change is constant.

PRESSURE SYSTEMS ━━━━━━━━━━━━━━━━━━━━━━━━━━━━━━━━━

We have already mentioned the creation of high pressure areas or systems on the surface. These areas are not stationary, but are free to move like a wave steered by the wind. In fact, the upper level winds—notably the jet stream—are the steering winds that control the action of pressure systems.

A high pressure system features winds that flow outward at the surface, inward at the top and downward (slowly) in the middle as shown in figure 36. As the air flows outward from the "high" at the surface, it turns to the right due to Coriolis effect so it ends up circulating clockwise around the center of the high. This is an important fact necessary to our understanding of weather and our ability to predict wind direction as we shall see.

Low pressure systems are secondary systems created by the upper air disturbances in the jet stream. The actual mechanism is beyond the scope of this book (see *Flying Conditions*), but we should know that although "lows" are secondary creations, they are primary weather makers. To understand this, we need to realize that the air moves inward at the bottom of a low, upward in the middle and outward at the top. This air too is turned rightward by Coriolis effect so that winds circulate counterclockwise around a low at the surface.

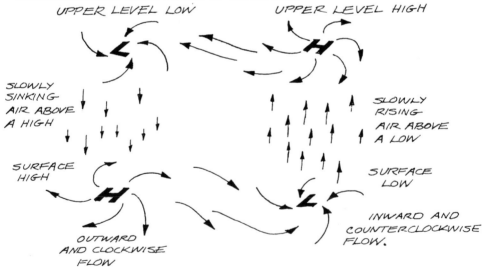

Figure 36 · Flow Patterns Around Pressure Systems

The slowly rising air in a low pressure system is cooled as it climbs because it expands due to decreasing pressure (expanding gases cool, contracting gases warm up). Any water vapor in the air eventually cools to its condensation point and thus forms tiny water droplets we see as cloud. Thus a low pressure system creates widespread clouds. On the other hand, a high pressure system with its sinking air typically evaporates all clouds and brings us those glorious sunny blue-sky days. Certain parts of our continent are famous for their high-dominated weather, while other areas are notorious for enduring a lot of lows with frequent clouds and rain.

FRONTAL SYSTEMS

Besides pressure systems, the other great items affecting our weather are fronts. Fronts are simply the boundary between cold air masses from the north and warm masses from the south. Since the air masses are driven by high pressure systems, the position of fronts themselves is largely determined by highs but is altered somewhat by the action of lows which often sit right on top of a front. Figure 37 shows this situation.

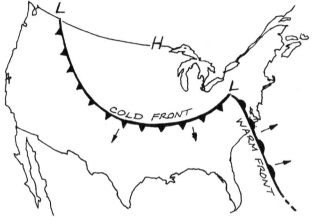

Figure 37 - Frontal and Pressure Systems

In the figure we have shown several types of fronts. The first is a cold front, the second a warm front and a third type is a stationary front. The only differences in these types is which air mass is advancing. If the cold air mass has a stronger high pressure system driving it, it will advance and the frontal boundary will move south as a cold front. Conversely, when the warm air mass is stronger it will move northward and the front is a warm front. When both masses are in a stalemate, we have a stationary front.

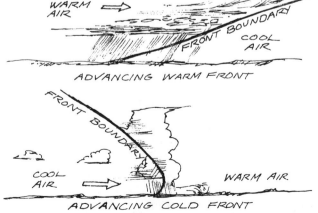

Figure 38 - Warm and Cold Fronts

47

Fronts are important to us because they bring changeable conditions. Wind shifts, turbulence, clouds and rain are associated with fronts. To see why, look at figure 38. Here we see that warm air rises above the cold air whether we have an advancing cold air mass (cold front) or warm mass (warm front). The result is a formation of clouds if any moisture is present, due to the rising air, just as in the vicinity of a low. Winds can shift as much as 180° from one side of a front to the other. Needless to say, we do not want to be flying in the vicinity of a strong passing front, so we must be able to recognize their signs or at least be aware of their approach from weather reports.

Clouds are, of course, an important sign of an approaching front. Study figure 38 and look at the different clouds associated with the different fronts. We'll learn to recognize these cloud types in the next section. Warm fronts often announce themselves well in advance—days perhaps—while cold front boundaries tend to be more abrupt.

CLOUD TYPES

We can separate clouds into two main types: stratus and cumulus. Stratus, like their Latin name implies are flat layered clouds. These often cover an entire sky and keep you indoors watching "Leave it to Beaver" reruns with their steady widespread rain. Cumulus clouds whose Latin name means accumulated, are tumbled puffy clouds that are often associated with fair weather and outdoor flying fun, but can sometimes develop into thunderstorms.

The two types of clouds differ in their development. All clouds are a result of lifting air. Stratus clouds occur when an entire layer of air is lifted as at the boundary of a warm front. Cumulus clouds occur when localized heating causes a warm mass of air to rise to the condensation level. In the lower atmosphere these rising masses are known as thermals and we shall learn more about them for they are very useful to us as pilots.

Besides the two main types of clouds, we also classify them as to their height. The very highest clouds are known as cirrus. The middle level clouds are called alto clouds with the lowest clouds having no particular prefex. Thus, we can talk of cirrus, cirrostratus and cirrocumulus clouds; altostratus and altocumulus clouds; and finally, stratus, cumulus and cummulostratus (a mixture) clouds. We also refer to nimbostratus and nimbocumulus clouds which simply means they are raining. The chart in figure 39 illustrates these different clouds and their relative heights. (Note, there are other types of clouds that we will encounter in our experience such as cap clouds, wave clouds and convergence clouds, but we'll discuss these when we discuss their cause).

It doesn't do more than make us encyclopedias if we can only recognize different cloud types. It is of great use if we can also make some predictions relating to our flying. So here are some generalities: Stratus clouds usually relate to stable conditions (see Chapter VIII). Stable conditions exhibit smooth air and not much lift other than ridge lift. (Note: at times stable air can exhibit turbulence in shear layers—see below). Cumulus clouds are formed in unstable conditions which means thermal turbulence and lift.

48

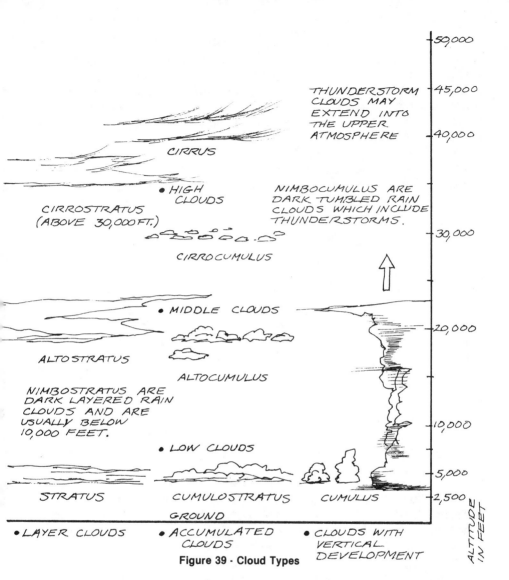

Figure 39 · Cloud Types

The lower the clouds, the more they tell on our immediate situation for the more likely we are to be in the influence of the air they adorn. Higher clouds may affect us only indirectly by blocking the sun or indicating an approaching front.

In any case, we must be observers of the sky and put our observations together with what we experience in flight to learn to predict our fate in the winds.

WATCHING THE WIND

We have learned that the creation of pressure systems and air mass movement largely determines our weather and the nature of the air we fly through. There is much available information on what to expect from the weather based on the movement of fronts and pressure systems. You can obtain this information from newspaper weather maps, television reports and Flight Service. Flight Service is available at airports and should be listed in your phone book under Federal Government listings. A paraglider is considered an ultralight vehicle in the US, so Flight Service is required to provide weather information to you. Ask them for significant winds and they will give you the speed and direction (in knots and degrees) at the surface and (usually) three and six thousand feet. Note: a knot is 1.15 miles per hour. Wind direction is given by the direction it is coming *from* as shown in figure 40. Degrees of a circle are used with zero starting at the north and continuing clockwise until 360° is again at the north. Thus, a 90° wind is an east wind (from the east). A northwest wind comes from the northwest or 315°.

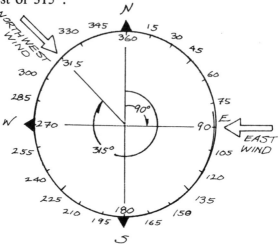

Figure 40 · Compass Rose

By now you should see that the pressure systems drive the wind. There is a general flow around the systems with a drift from high pressure to low pressure. By looking at a weather map you can predict the wind direction and strength from the relative placement of the pressure systems. An area between pressure systems will exhibit stronger winds as both the high and the low add their push and pull to the wind velocity. From observation you will note that winds after a cold front passes tend to blow from the west through north to northwest. Winds after a warm front passes tend to be southerly.

As a pilot we must learn to "watch" the wind. Of course, the wind is invisible so we can only watch its effects. However, with understanding and imagination we can begin to fathom the complixities of the airflow. Here's a handy tip: when trying to imagine the way the wind flows and interacts with the terrain and other obstructions imagine it to be water and draw on your experience of watching moving water swirl around rocks, logs and uneven banks in a stream.

There are three factors that concern us about the wind: its direction, velocity and turbulence or gustiness. We will look at each factor.

WIND DIRECTION _____

The wind direction is important for as we shall see in Chapter V, we must take off and land heading into the wind. We tell direction from natural causes such as blowing dust, moving leaves or grass and wind lines or ripples on water. Manmade items such as smoke and flags are ideal indicators of direction. Kicking up dust and dropping dried grass are two other traditional wind indicators used by pilots everywhere. Their drift gives you the direction as well as speed.

The best wind indicators are wind socks and streamers placed in visible positions at launch and in your landing area. Several such indicators grouped together allow you to watch the wind over a wide area. This is especially useful when the wind is changeable and you are approaching the ground to land.

WIND SPEED

Wind speed is of utmost concern to we pilots who fly with such little wings. If the wing is light we don't have much help on launch. If the wind is strong, we can get tossed like a butterfly in the breeze. Wind meters are the most reliable devices to use to determine the relative wind strength. However, you can also learn to judge wind speed by sound and feel. This ability takes some time to develop, but with a little practice you can achieve some fairly good educated guesses. Try closing your eyes, facing the wind and making a guess at the wind speed. Then consult a wind meter to correct your estimate. Eventually you will become a human walking wind meter.

Other sources of wind speed information are smoke stacks, cloud drift and trees. Figure 41 shows how stronger winds lays the smoke from a stack down more parallel with the ground. Clouds drift with the wind and give you a good idea of how fast the wind is blowing at their level. The movement of foliage and branches in trees are good indicators of wind strength to those who have experience observing such action. Windsocks, flags and streamers can also provide wind strength information through the angle of their dangle or the vigor of their flapping.

SMOKE IN STRONG, SMOOTH WIND

SMOKE IN TURBULENT WIND

SMOKE IN LIGHT WINDS

Figure 41 · Using Smoke as a Wind Indicator

51

The chart below will give you some guidelines for judging the wind strength by watching natural and manmade objects in the wind.

Wind Table	
Wind Velocity	Effects On Environment
calm	Smoke straight up. No movement in vegetation.
0-3 mph (0-5 km/h)	—Smoke straight up. Leaves begin to rustle.
3-5 mph (5-8 km/h)	—Smoke leans, twigs move.
5-10 mph (16-29 km/h)	—Smoke leans about 45°. Small branches and grass begin to move.
10-18 mph (16-29 km/h)	—Smoke lies about 30° up from horizontal. Whole branches begin moving. Grass waves. Clothes move on a line. Ridge soaring possible.
18-25 mph (29-40 km/h)	—Smoke lies flat. Large branches wave. Grass ripples and clothes wave. Dust swirls begin. Safe conditions only for very experienced pilots and only if smooth.
25-35 mph (40-56 km/h)	—Large limbs and medium trunks swag. Clothes flap. Dust and snow blow readily. Flying is very dangerous even for experienced pilots.
35 and over (56 km/h)	—Larger trees sway, cars rock. Difficulty walking into wind. Unsafe to fly a paraglider.

TURBULENCE

The last factor that characterizes the wind, turbulence, is perhaps the most important. If the wind is perfectly smooth, we can tolerate a much greater speed than we can if the wind is turbulent.

Turbulence is most often felt as gusts or changes in wind speed and direction when we are standing at launch or in the landing field. Our bodies and the action of an airspeed indicator (wind meter) are perhaps the best detectors of turbulence. Other things to watch are the action of smoke (see figure 41) and trees. Leaves and branches showing fast changes and wild action usually denote turbulent conditions.

In a later section we will discuss the causes of turbulence. Here we will close the topic by indicating the problem with turbulence is possible control problems, but more decidedly the possibility exists of collapsing a portion of your canopy in strong gusts. Needless to say, this can be dangerous near the ground.

You must learn to judge the degree of turbulence before you fly. To aid you in this judgement, remember this handy rule of thumb:

Of course, more experienced pilots can fly in more vigorous conditions than can beginners. However, the law of physics apply to even the seasoned eagle. At some point, no amount of experience or skill in the world will overcome the effects of powerful air. Learn to judge conditions carefully and fly well within the limits of safety.

THE WIND GRADIENT

Perhaps you have noticed that winds at the top of a hill or mountain are usually stronger than they are at the foot of the mountain. This variation of wind with altitude is known as wind gradient. Wind gradient has great importance in our flying, so we need to understand it in some detail.

When the wind blows over a rough surface such as the ground, it is slowed by the drag of objects in the path of the wind. Even a smooth surface such as a lake or sandy beach will slow the wind because of the interaction of the air's molecules with the surface irregularities. Thus, we should expect a wind gradient every time the wind blows.

Figure 42 depicts several possible wind gradient profiles. Note that the arrows indicating the wind show both direction and speed so they are drawn longer as height is gained. This is the wind gradient. Such a wind variation with altitude usually shows its greatest change in the lower 100 feet (30m). This is where we take off and land, so we need to be aware of the presence of a wind gradient.

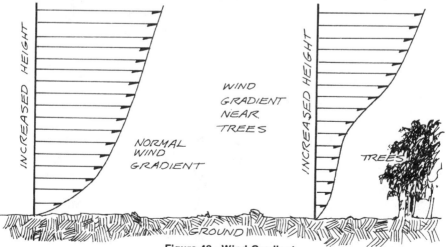

Figure 42 · Wind Gradient

In Chapter V we will investigate how to land in a wind gradient. For now we should understand that landing into a wind gradient can cause a stall if we do not have enough airspeed as we descend into a decreased headwind. The slow speed of paragliders make them particularly susceptible to such wind gradient problems since the change in wind velocity may be a significant portion of our flying speed. The simple cure is to speed up when descending close to the ground. For precise landing technique in a wind gradient, please see Chapter V.

Another problem presented by the wind gradient is the chance to encounter higher winds if we get lifted aloft. The art of using lift is detailed in Chapter IX, but for now be aware that if the winds are not low enough for you to launch at the top of your hill, you may find lower winds on the slope below. However, if the wind is strong enough to carry you upward, you may encounter winds too strong to penetrate as you climb. It is considered bad form to hang your laundry out across the countryside, so be aware of the wind gradient effects and take this into account when flying in winds of any velocity.

DAILY VARIATIONS

The sun has proven to be the main engine that sets our planet's atmosphere to swirling. We will find another more direct effect of the sun: the daily variation in wind velocity.

When a front isn't in the process of passing through, we recognize that winds are normally lighter at night and stronger during the day. The reason for this is the sun heats the lower levels of the atmosphere by warming the earth's surface. This produces a mixing of the air which brings the upper level winds down to the surface. We get stronger winds during the day because the wind gradient is partially negated.

At night, the reverse is true. The earth cools as it radiates heat into outer space. This cools the air immediately above the surface creating a cold, dense layer that is moved little by the upper winds. We often encounter still air at night as the gradient intensifies.

When we are near uneven terrain—mountains, hills or even sloping ground—the daily wind variations are exaggerated. During the day the sun's heating tends to warm the air at the surface so it flows upward along a slope. Figure 43(a) shows how these upward flowing winds are present near the surface (typically less than 100 ft from the slope). In the valleys or low areas the air is usually sinking to replace the air flowing toward the slope and upward.

At night the reverse is true. As the surface cools, the air it contacts becomes cooler also and slides down the slope since it is denser and heavier as shown in figure 43(b). We have several names for these winds. Upslope winds are also called valley winds or anabatic flow. Downslope winds are known as mountain winds, gravity winds or catabatic flow.

The change from upslope to downslope winds takes place nearly every day the sun is shining. In fact the only time it doesn't occur is when the general widespread flow is in an opposing direction and of sufficient strength to bully the less robust slope winds.

This daily variation usually occurs at a slow pace, with upslope winds peaking in velocity in the early afternoon and dying by nightfall to be replaced by a gradually building downslope breeze that in turn stops and reverses in the morning sun.

However, sometimes the changes can be dramatic. Occasionally, in mountain areas, canyons can store cool air as evening falls that breaks out suddenly into the flat areas. This can result in a complete reversal of the wind in a landing area within a second or two. Some gusty conditions may accompany such a reversal, but the main problem is the possibility of landing downwind.

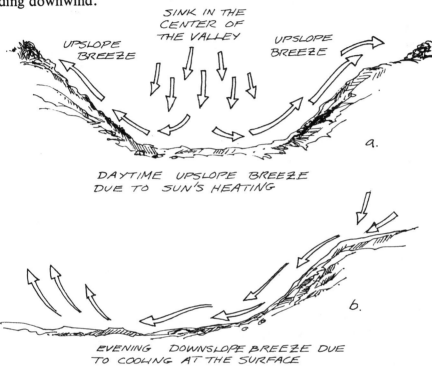

DAYTIME UPSLOPE BREEZE
DUE TO SUN'S HEATING

EVENING DOWNSLOPE BREEZE DUE
TO COOLING AT THE SURFACE

Figure 43 · Daily Wind Variation

When flying in mountainous areas, you can prevent great embarassment by carefully monitoring your landing field windsock during those late afternoon, early evening flights. Sensitive wind streamers do not lie. Heavier socks may not respond to an abrupt wind change, especially, if they are wet with dew. Think about it.

LAND AND SEA BREEZES

A special type of daily wind variation occurs near large bodies of water (the Great Lakes or the oceans). As shown in figure 44a, during the day the sun heats the land surface much more than the water. The air becomes heated over the land and rises as it expands and lowers in density. The cool air over the water then moves towards the land to replace the rising air. The warm air aloft moves seaward to replace the depleting cool air. In this manner a circulation is set up that continues as long as the sun shines. This circulation is known as the sea breeze.

A sea breeze can be quite strong and reach inland as much as 30 miles (48 km) when desert areas are near the sea as in the American Southwest.

However, more typically the seabreeze winds are less than 15 mph (24 km/h) and extends only 10 miles (16 km) or so inland.

As evening falls, the land cools and the water becomes the warmer body since water has a huge heat capacity. As a result, the circulation reverses with a breeze blowing from the land to the sea known as a land breeze as shown in figure 44b.

There are two effects of the sea breeze we need to consider. The first is the creation of smooth, steady winds near the sea on most days. These winds may be ideal for learning to ridge soar a paraglider if the velocity is reasonable. The second effect is the possibility of the seabreeze reaching inland and reversing the direction of the general wind. This often occurs at coastal sites and a classic example is the area around Lake Elsinore, Ca. Here pilots of all forms of aviation expect a wind reversal in the surrounding hills by early afternoon.

One final point to note when dealing with these local circulations is the possibility of a circulation of air between any warm and cool areas located adjacent to one another. It is not uncommon to see a light wind drifting from a cool forest area to a warm area of fields or crops. We mention this phenomena as an explanation rather than a matter of concern in our flying.

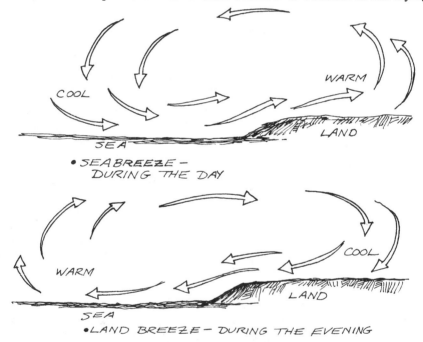

COOL

WARM

LAND

SEA

• SEABREEZE —
DURING THE DAY

WARM

COOL

LAND

SEA

• LAND BREEZE — DURING THE EVENING

Figure 44 · Land and Sea Breezes

TURBULENCE—WASHBOARD AIR

Throughout this discussion of the sky's habits, we have alluded to turbulence more than once. That is because we find texture in the air more often than not. Let us investigate this all-important matter.

We will define turbulence as any sudden change in the air that is felt as a gust at launch or a tug on our canopy in flight. Turbulence can best be understood as a series of random swirls or eddies in the air, although in the case of thermals and wing vortices, the swirling is quite organized.

Turbulence can be separated into four types for our purposes. They are: mechanical, thermal, shear and wake turbulence. A brief description of each type is in order. Later (in Chapter VI) we will go into more detail on the dangers and handling of turbulence.

MECHANICAL TURBULENCE

Mechanical turbulence results when wind passes over and around solid objects on the ground. You can visualize this type of turbulence by watching water swirl around rocks in a stream. The faster the flow and the larger the obstructions, the greater the swirls created in both the stream and the air. Figure 45 shows how the swirls created by an obstruction vary with object size and sharpness. We can also see how the swirls gradually break up to smaller swirls and die out downstream from the source of disturbance.

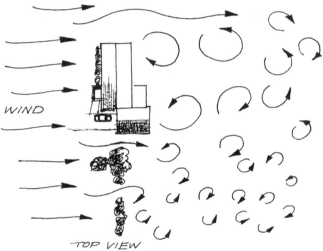

Figure 45 · Mechanical Turbulence

We should always expect some mechanical turbulence close to the ground in any wind. Some objects such as houses, tree lines or hills may exhibit a turbulent swirl that stays in one place behind them in certain wind conditions. This is known as a rotor and can be seen in your favorite stream as well as in figure 46. To avoid such turbulence we establish the following rule:

Avoiding Mechanical Turbulence
In order to avoid turbulence, the distance to land downwind of an object measured in number of heights of the object is equal to the velocity of the wind in miles per hour times the object height. That is, D (the downwind distance) = V (wind velocity in mph) × H (the object height). For example, if the wind is 10 mph, land 10 times the height of an object away from that object.

Figure 46 · Rotors

THERMAL TURBULENCE

Thermal turbulence occurs when warm bubbles of air form on the earth's surface then rise like a hot air balloon. They disturb the air as they pass and can feel like strong bumps when we fly through them. They are the classic aviation "air pocket." See figure 47.

Thermals can readily occur when there is no general wind movement, so light wind days aren't alway glossy smooth. When a thermal lifts off it sucks air inward beneath it, so the presence of thermals can usually be detected by noting changing wind directions at launch or in the landing area.

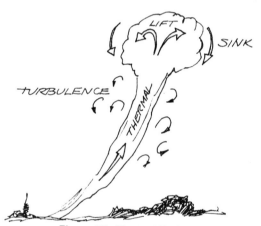

Figure 47 · Thermal Turbulence

SHEAR TURBULENCE

Shear turbulence occurs when two different air masses rub against each other. This often happens at frontal boundaries, but can also occur when a valley fills with cool air in the evening while warmer air moves above this cool air. The warm air rubbing over the cooler, denser air produces swirls at the interface as shown in figure 48. Be aware of the possibility of such turbulent layers when flying in the evening in closed valleys.

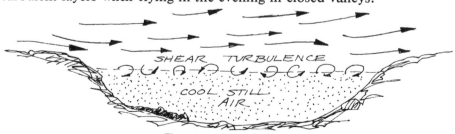

Figure 48 · Shear Turbulence

58

WAKE TURBULENCE

The final form of turbulence is wake turbulence produced by a passing aircraft. In figure 49 we have drawn a hang glider producing wake turbulence since this is the type of aircraft we are most likely to encounter. As shown in the figure, wake turbulence consists of some random swirls, but mainly of two large rotating vortices emanating from the wing tips. To avoid such turbulence, avoid flying directly behind another aircraft. It is especially important not to land directly behind another aircraft for vortices are stronger when they are flying slowly (as when landing) and strong turbulence near the ground is never welcome.

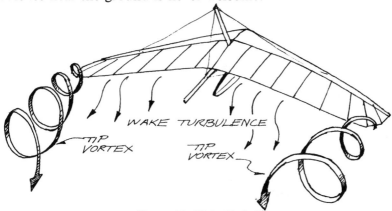

Figure 49 · Wake Turbulence

As mentioned previously, the problem presented by turbulence is perhaps a slight loss of control, but most definitely a possibility of canopy collapse. We will see in Chapter VI how to deal with canopy deflation due to turbulence, but for now we must be conscious to limit our flying to relatively smooth conditions.

THUNDERSTORMS—AERIAL MONSTERS

One last important feature in the sky is the threat to all aviation: thunderstorms. Thunderstorms are formed when humid air is heated and convects upward to form a large cloud mass. The vigorous action of updrafts and falling rain in the large cloud produces violent swirls and electrical imbalance that results in lightning. As a thunderstorm matures, it drops its load of moisture to create downdrafts and gusty winds.

In figure 50 we see the birth, growth and maturity of a thunderstorm. In the later stages of development a thunderstorm is dangerous indeed. These dangers are: Strong updrafts that may suck you into the cloud where lack of visibility may cause vertigo and loss of control as well as lifting you to altitudes where you cannot survive due to lack of oxygen (thunderstorm clouds often reach over the 50,000 ft level). Downdrafts occur that can slam you to the ground and produce gust fronts that exhibit extreme winds as much as ten miles in front of the thunderstorm. If those dangers aren't enough to daunt you, there is the distinct possibility of freezing to death in the upper levels, dying from a lighting strike or getting pounded by golf ball hail.

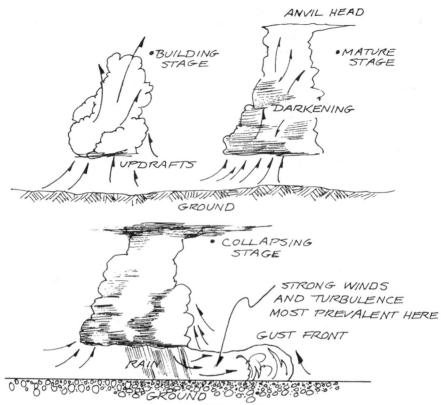

Figure 50 · Thunder Storms

The severity of a thunderstorm can be foretold somewhat by the size of the forming cloud, the vertical cloud buildup and the darkness of the cloud. The larger, taller and darker a cloud is, the more danger it represents. Unfortunately, in humid areas, thunderstorms can be imbedded in a general haze layer which precludes detecting their nature or presence. Thunder may be the only indicator that they are around and in any case, thunder indicates lighting which in turn indicates the storm is mature and should be avoided like the killer it is. Thunderstorms and aviation are not compatible. Don't fly in their presence.

SUMMARY

We pilots of light and slow aircraft must be intimately aware of the ways of the wind. As we make our way through the sky we need to study, observe and feel the three-dimensional flow of air. Safe flying demands an understanding of general weather patterns so we can choose the reasonable days and also demands insight into the small-scale effects so we can avoid danger areas and surprises.

Our knowledge of turbulence, its causes and likely whereabouts must be highly developed. Likewise our thunderstorm awareness. Once we have acquired such knowledge and skill, then we can begin to concentrate more on using the air to our personal benefit. When the halls of the sky are as familiar as those of our own home, then we will truly belong with the creatures of the air.

CHAPTER V

Learning To Fly
Beginner Skills

Now here's the part you've been waiting for. This is where you actually learn to fly after all your anticipation and background study.

In this lesson we will follow the outline of the American Paragliding Association training program, for this program is designed to teach flying in a safe, gradual manner. Take your time and learn each phase of training thoroughly with the help of your instructor, for this is where the basics are acquired that will serve you well throughout your flying career.

Before we can get a taste of the sky we must discuss a few more items. The first is you, the pilot. As you recall, the pilot is the third part of our wing, wind and windividual triad. After we check our gear and the conditions, we must check ourselves.

PREPARING THE PILOT

A typical paragliding training course lasts four or more days. During that short period you will be inundated with new information and sensations. It is normal to experience a period of doubt whether or not you can truly master all that's presented. This doubt is soon dispelled as you gain knowledge a little bit at a time and build skills that soon become automatic.

Any fear of failure or heights you have will likewise be dispelled for you'll find that the necessary skills will come in a few trials and you'll learn to trust your instructor, your equipment and yourself.

To perform your best, however, you should be properly prepared. To begin, you should dress in protective clothing (long pants) as per your instructor's directions or the guidelines in Chapter II. You will probably be supplied with a helmet, but other items of dress are your own responsibility (gloves, boots or running shoes, etc.).

Your physical and emotional state are the most important factors you bring to the schooling situation. You will be out in the sun lugging your body up and down hills. If that body has a bit of extra cargo on board, your job will be a little harder, and you must pace yourself. Don't push yourself too hard for the effects of adrenaline mask the feeling of fatigue until it sets in suddenly with a vengence. Your instructor is aware of this phenomenon, but you are the best monitor of your physical state. Take frequent rests and pay attention to your condition.

You should have a good breakfast the day you take lessons. Your body needs fuel to replace the energy stores you will be tapping with your mental and physical exertion. Bring a lunch and plenty of liquid too, if the lesson lasts the day.

Needless to say, drugs and alcohol do not mix with flying. Conventional pilots have a rule that states: eight hours from bottle to throttle. We can alter that with poetic license to apply to paragliding: *eight hours from bottle to toggles.* Learning to fly with a hangover from the previous night's revelry can slow your progress and make a serious dent in your fun.

There are many drugs besides recreational drugs that can impair your performance. Antihistamines are known to reduce mental acuity and even aspirin has been implicated in aviation accidents. Any illness such as a cold or the flu will reduce your ability to perform and is cause for cancelling your lesson. Don't be impatient, the wind and the hills aren't going on vacation.

Of particular importance in regard to flying is your emotional state. If your mind is otherwise occupied by such things as the loss of someone close to you or if you just told your boss to find another lackey, then you cannot give total attention to the necessity of learning flying skills. You should carefully assess your emotional situation and if you feel you are not 100%, have your sympathetic instructor postpone the lesson. Certainly it is a legitimate thought to take up a new pursuit such as paragliding to help you forget past problems, but you should not be attempting to fly if these problems are so recent that they overwhelm your mental awareness. This advice should be heeded throughout your flying career as well as in the early training period.

The most important factor concerning you, the pilot, is your attitude. We're not equating you to the kid in the back row of English class shooting spitballs at the teacher, for learning to fly is rewarding, challenging and fun. What we are referring to is an attitude of safety that must be developed from the first day on the hill to serve you well throughout your continued flying experience. A certain amount of willingness to try new things is a prerequisite to becoming a competent pilot. However, you must learn and respect the limits. These limits are imposed by the forces of nature and your own experience level. You cannot dublicate the feats of more practiced pilots until you have paid your dues by accumulating airtime in safe situations. Remember:

> *"There are old pilots and there are bold pilots but there are no old, bold pilots."*

THE IDEAL SITE

Without a doubt your instructor will have the training hill already selected and prepared. However, to further your understanding and for your use when you are on your own, we will describe the perfect site.

The shape of any training hill should include a gentle transition from flat ground to the actual slope (see figure 51). The ideal angle of slope is from 20° to 30° which is about equivalent to a 2.5 to 1 and a 1.5 to 1 glide ratio respectively. Any flatter than this, and you may have trouble getting airborne; any steeper and the launch may be intimidating for a beginner.

Of course, the slope should face the prevailing wind and be unobstructed for a long distance upwind (say ½ mile), both to minimize turbulence and remove the chance of landing on non-standard spots like trees, houses, or cars. Make sure your hill is clear *behind* the takeoff area also in case of a blowback.

The ideal slope should be grassy and smooth with no rocks or ruts to twist an ankle or trip you during takeoff or landing for at least 15 paces. A "double bump" hill as shown in the figure can be very dangerous for you may not have enough performance to clear the lower hump and yet not have enough airspeed to land on it properly.

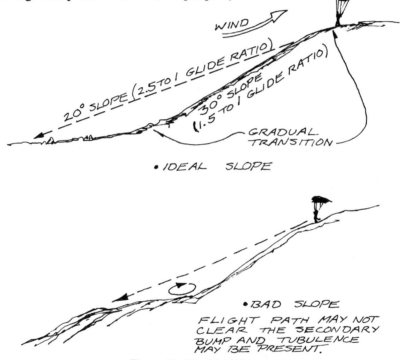

Figure 51 · The Ideal Slope

A decrease in the steepness of a slope along your run path can also be a problem, for as you level out you relax pressure on the front risers which may result in the front of your canopy collapsing or folding under if you are running slowly. This will immediately deflate the entire canopy and stop your takeoff action. You can experiment with different slopes to learn the best shapes.

Here are two other matters that bear consideration. First, it is desirable for your training hill to be isolated so as not to attract distracting spectators. You should even discourage your friends or family from coming to watch your beginning flying experience for they often demand your attention and worse, tempt you to perform.

Next, you should obtain permission to use any site you intend to fly. Some sites are established hang gliding sites and you must understand the standard rules or you may lose the site priviledges for yourself and the rest of the flying community. This is not the way to popularize our sport.

Most landowners in the U.S. are extremely worried about liability. That's not unreasonable considering the litigation lottery that prevails here. The best way to handle this state of affairs is to show the landowner your liability insurance (you get this automatically when you join the APA) and offer to sign a waiver. Have a waiver ready when you meet the landowner and your way will be greatly smoothed. We provide for you an example of a very powerful waiver in Appendix III of this book.

FLYING CONDITIONS

Now we have described the ideal site, let's define the ideal conditions. Naturally we want the wind to be blowing straight into the hill so we can launch directly into it. If the wind is blowing crosswise to our intended run, it will blow the canopy to the side. If it is from our rear, it will require much more running in order to gain flying airspeed. A tailwind of any significant strength is dangerous and will make it impossible to launch. We normally launch and land directly into the wind to minimize our groundspeed.

Zero wind is acceptable after the first day's lesson, but will require much more running to effect a takeoff. Without wind, the pre-takeoff in-air check of the canopy is much more difficult while line-overs and end cell closures are more common (these terms are explained in a later section). Calm wind launches increase the pilot attention requirements.

The ideal wind velocity is 5 to 8 mph (8 to 13 km/h). The steeper your hill, the lighter wind you can tolerate. Of course, this wind should be smooth with no sudden changes of velocity or direction. If changes do occur, they should be gradual and within the above velocity limits.

We have described the ideal site and conditions for the training situation, but let's be realistic: the ideals cannot always be met. How much can we compromise? Here are our absolute operating limits:

Operating Limits For Training
- Wind Speed—12 mph (19 km/h) maximum (5-8 mph ideal)
- Wind Direction—30° cross maximum (straight in ideal)
- Wind Gust Factor—3 mph (5 km/h) change in 10 seconds maximum (no change ideal)
- Slope Angle—A minimum of 20° (2.5 to 1 glide ratio) in wind (30° ideal)

CAUTION: It is not uncommon to experience an upslope wind when, in fact, the true wind is blowing over the back of the hill. The reason for this is a rotor often exists on the downwind side of a hill, especially if the slope is steep and the hill is high. Be very careful not to mistake a rotor for a good upslope wind, for launching into a rotor will put you through a gauntlet of sink and strong turbulence as shown in figure 52. Check the overall wind direction by using the signs outlined in Chapter IV long before you climb your hill. Also, check the backside of your hill if possible for signs of a contrary wind. 64

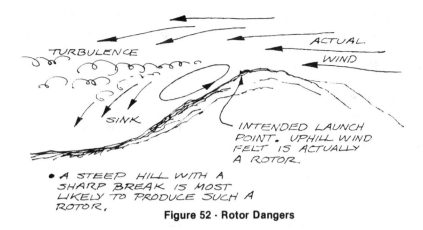

TURBULENCE

ACTUAL
WIND

SINK

INTENDED LAUNCH
POINT. UPHILL WIND
FELT IS ACTUALLY
A ROTOR.

● A STEEP HILL WITH A
SHARP BREAK IS MOST
LIKELY TO PRODUCE SUCH A
ROTOR.

Figure 52 · Rotor Dangers

LAYING OUT THE CANOPY

Now it's time to let the cat or rather the bird out of the bag. Orient yourself near your takeoff position (for a beginner this will be on the flat ground) and determine the wind direction (there should be plenty of wind streamers at your site to announce the wind's character). Pull your glider out of its pack and unravel the lines to place the harness upwind of the canopy as shown in figure 53a.

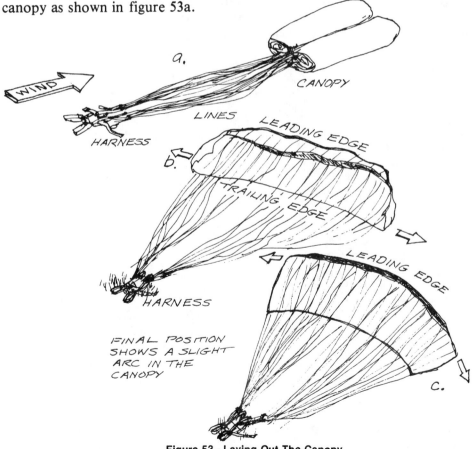

a.

WIND

CANOPY

LINES

HARNESS

LEADING EDGE

b.

TRAILING EDGE

HARNESS

FINAL POSITION
SHOWS A SLIGHT
ARC IN THE
CANOPY

LEADING EDGE

c.

Figure 53 · Laying Out The Canopy

At this point we are assuming light winds and the presence of assistants. In the next chapter we will see what to do in the absence of these luxuries.

The next step is to lay the canopy *flat on its back* in a pre-selected smooth area. Two ground crew members should unroll the canopy or take the two trailing edge corners (one each) and walk out to spread the canopy and pull it tight (see figure 53b). They then take the leading edge corners and spread the back of the canopy to lie it flat (53c). A slight crown or arc in the canopy with the ends placed closer to the pilot than the center is a good practice since the lines in the center are longer.

While this process is going on, you should lift the harness off the ground so the harness and lines are not being dragged. Remember, that the most frequent damage occurs to a glider from ground contact.

PREFLIGHTING

Once the canopy is stretched out, lay the harness down upwind of the canopy with the front lines stretched out. From the minute the glider is removed from the pack, you should be handling it and checking for damage or problems. At this point you must do a serious overall inspection known in aviation circles as a preflight.

There are two facets of a proper preflight: 1. *Attention to detail* and 2. *following a complete routine.* This method assures that you inspect every item carefully. Remember, the purpose of a preflight is to make sure your wing is sound *before* it becomes your life support. Here are the steps to a proper preflight:

Preflight Check List

1. Look at entire canopy for tears, punctures or abrasions. Check for pulled or missing stitching. Look under the canopy to pay special attention to the top surface.
2. Check the canopy for sand, gravel or small rocks. Even a small amount of these items in the canopy can affect its flying characteristics.
3. Check each line for continuity, tangles and abrasion. Clear all lines from sticks and each other.
4. Check the line-to-riser connections (rapid links).
5. Make sure the steering lines are secure to the toggles and routed freely through the guide rings.
6. Check the harness for abrasions and pulled stitching.
If any one of these checks indicate a problem, correct it if possible or abort your flight.

To clear the lines, lift the harness by one of the front risers and shake to see if the lines connected to this riser are straight and untangled. Hold the riser with your inside hand and pull the outside (corner) line away from the other lines with your other hand. If this line is routed properly, the other lines on this side should be proper. This check is intended to make sure that your harness didn't get twisted through the lines during packing or unpacking. Note: the corner front lines go to the leading edge corners. If the front lines are clear, generally all the lines will be clear.

After checking the rear lines routed to the rear risers, check the steering lines on both sides. Hold the steering line above its keeper or guide on the riser and pull it completely to the side with your free hand. It should come from underneath all the other lines and lie clear of them as well as any rocks, brush or sticks (see figure 54). Repeat this process for the other side. You are now ready for the next step.

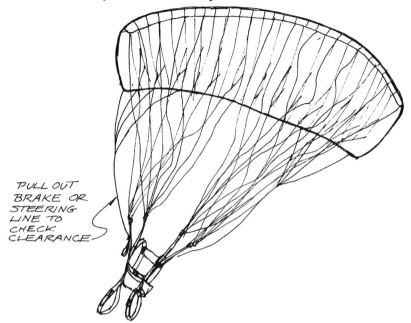

PULL OUT BRAKE OR STEERING LINE TO CHECK CLEARANCE

Figure 54 · Checking the Steering Lines

GROUND HANDLING—CANOPY INFLATION

Now its time to don your gear. Put your helmet on first for you'll feel awkward trying to retrieve your helmet if you've already strapped in to your harness. Next comes the harness. There are two main types of entry. The sling harness requires you to put your legs through the leg loops first then buckle up the waist and chest straps (see figure 7). The seat harness is put on your shoulders first then the individual leg loops are fastened.

In both cases, hold the harness in front of you and again check to make sure it is not flipped through itself, then turn around and enter the harness without twisting it or pulling the lines. Your instructor's assistance will be welcome here the first couple times you perform this feat. Once your harness is on, adjust it by tightening the straps until they are snug.

While you are climbing into your harness your assistants have been holding the canopy and are now ready to help you lift the canopy. You are the pilot in command (although your instructor will tell you what to do initially) and they will obey your declarations. Your commands to them will be "READY CANOPY" and "LIFT" at the appropriate time. The ground crew procedures will be outlined in the next section.

Now you should proceed to lifting mode. First make sure that no lines are caught on your harness buckles or your helmet. Next, put your hands through the steering toggles with the rear risers on your forearms as shown in figure 55. The best way to do this without getting confused is to start at the harness with the rear riser, run your hand along it away from the harness to clear it from the other risers, then place it over your arm. Repeat this procedure with the next, more forward riser.

Your arms should be in back of all risers as shown. Now grasp the front risers with your thumb at the back and fingers in front as shown in the detail. It is important that *no slack is allowed between the harness and your grip on the front risers.*

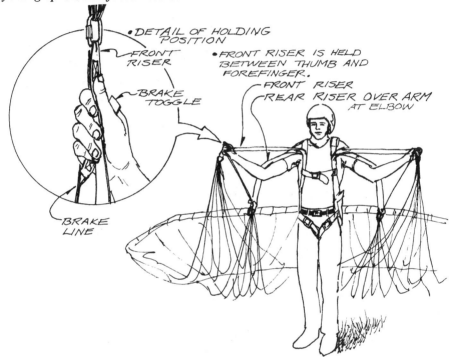

Figure 55 · Positioning the Risers

At this point you must check the wind conditions. If the breeze is smooth and straight toward you then all systems are go. Assume the position. This is a crucifix posture as shown in figure 56. Note that your elbows may be slightly bent, but there *must not be slack in the risers from hand to harness.*

Position yourself directly on the centerline of the canopy and forward of the trailing edge so the lines to the leading edge are just beginning to tighten. You can rustle these lines to tease the canopy and feel the proper position (see figure 57).

Now with your feet in a position to provide acceleration (one foot forward with weight on the balls), lean your body slightly forward with your head and eyes directly upward. The front risers should still be tight from chest to hand and you should feel a slight amount of tension in the lines that goes to the corners of the leading edge. With your instructor's approval, give the command to ready canopy and wait for the reply "canopy

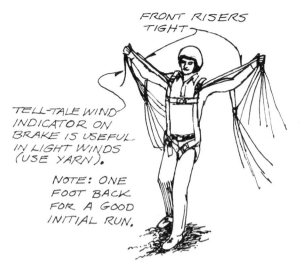

FRONT RISERS TIGHT

TELL-TALE WIND INDICATOR ON BRAKE IS USEFUL IN LIGHT WINDS (USE YARN).

NOTE: ONE FOOT BACK FOR A GOOD INITIAL RUN.

Figure 56 · Takeoff Position

ready." As soon as you hear this, yell "LIFT!" and move forward immediately while moving your arms forward and up. If you do everything properly, the canopy should lift behind you and rise to float over your head.

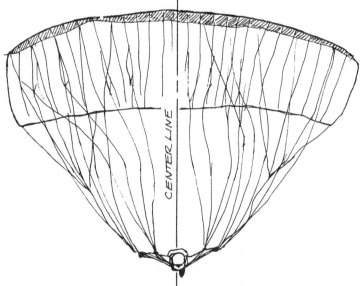

CENTER LINE

Figure 57 · Top View of Takeoff Position

The proper lifting action may take a few practice runs and is shown in figure 58. Try for a good clean, continuous pull up and drive through until the canopy inflates. Possible errors are shown in the figure. Dropping the head tends to lower the arms and prevents you from checking the canopy. Failure to keep the arms pulling straight out and up will result in a non-inflation. Pulling on the brakes will likewise prevent inflation.

As the canopy inflates above you, you must let go of the front risers. At

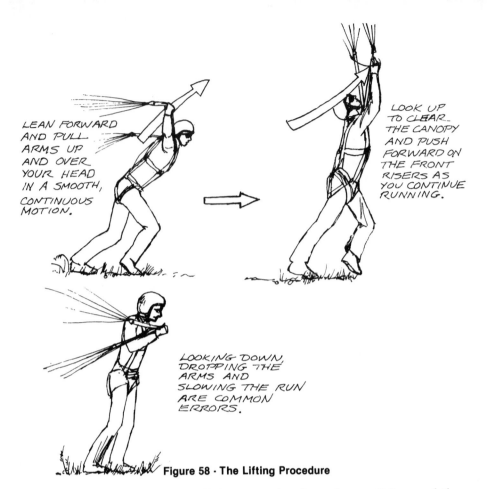

LEAN FORWARD AND PULL ARMS UP AND OVER YOUR HEAD IN A SMOOTH, CONTINUOUS MOTION.

LOOK UP TO CLEAR THE CANOPY AND PUSH FORWARD ON THE FRONT RISERS AS YOU CONTINUE RUNNING.

LOOKING DOWN, DROPPING THE ARMS AND SLOWING THE RUN ARE COMMON ERRORS.

Figure 58 · The Lifting Procedure

this stage you should never pull down on the risers, but pull forward then ease your grip as they begin pulling upward. As you release the risers, your hands should move forward to prepare to use the brakes. You must look up and stop the canopy directly over your head with a slight application of brakes. This constitutes a proper inflation.

Once the canopy is inflated, you must *always* perform a canopy check by looking up and back (do not turn around) as shown in figures 58 and 61. This canopy check is essential to insure proper inflation and line routing. Generally, you can perform this check while standing still, for the canopy will float its weight in just a few miles per hour wind. However, in calm conditions you must perform this check while running.

Common malfunctions during inflations are line entanglements, line overs and end-cell closures. The first two may be remedied by plucking the offending lines. End-cell closures are a result of an incomplete inflation at the canopy ends. The remedy here is to vigorously pump both brakes to increase the internal canopy pressure. Often speeding up your run will do the same trick, however, on critical launches it is better to abort takeoff than risk entering the air with a malfunction.

The best way to prevent malfunctions is to lay the canopy out carefully to begin with. Make sure the end lines are on *top* of the canopy. Jiggle the lines free and remove all sticks from the area. Finally, make sure the canopy is spread symmetrically with the center cells open to inflate first.

Here your instructor may let you feel the canopy by holding your harness while you make slight steering controls and experience the harness tug. At this point you should begin to learn to stabilize the canopy by using the brakes to keep it directly over your head. If the canopy moves to the side, pull the brake on the opposite side to turn the canopy slightly so that it flies back over your head. You can also try moving to the side under the canopy if it gets blown to the side. This can only be done of course if your launch site is wide enough to allow plenty of clearance.

If the canopy moves forward or back you can adjust its position by pulling down on the brakes or the front risers respectively. If your hands are operating the brakes, you should put them back on the front risers to push for taking off. In any case, you should learn to feel the position of your canopy and learn to anticipate the proper correcting control input long before your canopy gets too far out of position. Practice this to perfection.

Another exercise you may eventually try is to turn in the harness to face

A good, vigorous launch run, but note the end-cell closure on the pilot's left wing.

The pilot collapses the canopy off to the side by pulling one brake.

71

the canopy before lifting it and controlling its position by pulling on the front risers individually. With this procedure you do not put your hands in the toggles until you turn back to face forward. This practice is an important procedure when you are launching in wind by yourself and allows you to check the canopy carefully before commencing to aviate. Of course, this technique requires a certain minimum wind. In Chapter VI we look at such reverse launches in detail.

Now you can deflate the canopy to repeat your lift practice. To effect this deflation, simply pull both brake controls as far down and forward as you can. This action will stall the wing and it will drop behind you. An alternate method is to pull one brake line totally down so that the canopy turns and drops on its side behind you. This is useful for packing the canopy. In an emergency, pulling hard on any line will serve to collapse the canopy.

Canopy Collapse Procedures

•Pull both brakes as far as possible.
•Pull one brake as far as possible.
•Pull both rear risers as far as possible.
•Pull any line as far as possible *in an emergency*.

Naturally you will want to repeat these ground handling procedures over and over until you can inflate a canopy every time. After each inflation remember to look up to check the canopy. This is called a *flight check*.

Rocks, sand, sticks or used tires stuck to the canopy will alter its flying ability and render it unsafe (we're just joking about the tires, the rest is real). A line routed over the end of the canopy (known as a lineover) or a collapsed end cell (end cell closure) can ruin your day if not your whole week. Do not take off with these malfunctions; shake them loose or abort the flight by collapsing the canopy.

It should be clear that no-wind takeoffs are more demanding for the simple reason that you must make these flight checks by looking back over your head while running down hill!

Flight Check List

Check For:
•Debris and foreign objects stuck to the canopy or lines.
•Lines routed over the canopy.
•End cell closures.

GROUND CREW PROCEDURES

While you're having fun lofting the canopy into the air, your assistants or ground crew are attending to their duties. Their main job is to prevent the wind from blowing the canopy around and to aid your canopy lift. This is their procedure: While you are getting into your gear, the ground crew pair has been holding the glider's trailing edge out tautly to prevent the wind from blowing it away. They have been stationed here from the time the canopy is laid out, for even in no apparent wind a thermal gust can spring up.

Once you are strapped in with your harness adjusted, they are listening to your commands for they know you are in control and in the most vulnerable position in high winds. If they are inexperienced they should be reminded that there is a person strapped in the harness.

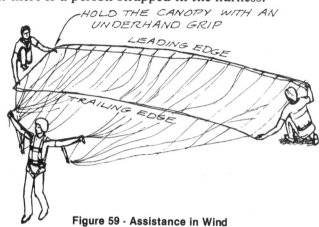

Figure 59 - Assistance in Wind

On your "READY" command, they reach back with their rear hand to grasp the leading edge with an *underhand* grip as shown in figure 59. In a wind the crew must continue to hold the trailing edge tightly to the ground. If there is no wind (for certain), they may both kneel behind the canopy and use both hands on the leading edge as in figure 60. They should be on one knee ready to stand up as shown. Once they are in position they announce "CANOPY READY!" and await your command.

When you shout "LIFT!" the crew stands straight up while lifting their arms straight up and letting go of the canopy at the maximum height. This lifting procedure takes about one second. If they are positioned as in figure 59, they naturally release the trailing edge as they lift the leading edge with their rear hand.

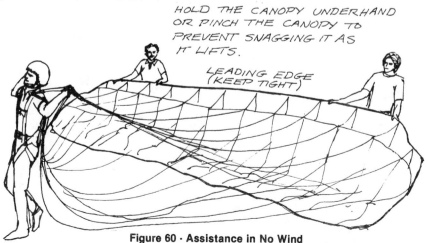

Figure 60 - Assistance in No Wind

73

The ground crew must be instructed to lift the canopy straight up—*don't* run forward and *don't* throw it into the air. Hold it underhanded to allow a smooth release. Both crew members must release the canopy at the same moment (it helps if they are watching one another). They will create a problem if one holds on longer than the other for the canopy will be turned as it tries to inflate. They should have in mind the rule: when in doubt, let go.

INTO THE AIR

It is time for your first launch. Here's how its going to be:

> ### Your First Launch
>
> *You strap into the harness, position yourself with the risers in your hand and listen to your instructor's last minute reminders. Now it's just you and the wind along with that vague impression of a living creature behind you seeming to wait for your command to take to the sky.*
>
> *You check the wind and your lines one more time and you realize everything is in perfect order. It's time to commit aviation.*
>
> *You feel excitement and just a little fear. That fear is natural for anyone performing what seems like an unnatural act for the first time. But you have been programmed for success by your instructor's careful guidance, your reading and step by step practice. Your fear subsides as your self-confidence assures you that you're ready.*
>
> *With a command "LIFT!" you propel yourself forward and look up to see your canopy inflating above you. A quick check proves everything is in order. You lean forward and accelerate the canopy to top speed by pushing on the risers with your hands or arms. As you continue running you get lighter and lighter, then suddenly you're airborne!*
>
> *By now your hands are off the risers and holding the control toggles near your shoulders. You look around and can hardly believe you are flying. You don't have much time for sightseeing though. The ground is coming back to greet you and it's time to think about landing. You release the brakes for speed then give them a smooth full pull to stop the canopy and you land with a light step.*
>
> *You collapse the canopy then look back with a grin at your take off. It isn't all that far away, but it sure felt as if you soared like an eagle! "What a rush," you think as you gather the canopy for the trek back up hill. "I've got to do that again!" And you will, for all your preparation has rewarded you with the foundation to build your skills to a highly tuned level. Welcome to the family of sky adventurers.*

Before you can experience this magic we must cover a few details. To begin, we will separate the takeoff into two phases, although in reality the action is a smooth transition from standing still to flying.

The first phase is canopy inflation including canopy check. You know how to do this, you've practiced it many times. The second phase is acceleration to takeoff speed. If you recall, the flying speeds of any wing are dependent on its wing loading. The canopy only needs 5 mph (8 km/h) or so to inflate and lift its own weight. However, to lift you it needs more airspeed. You must give it this airspeed by accelerating yourself and the canopy to at least 12 mph (19 km/h) relative to the air.

A pilot accelerates and lifts to inflate.

Here's the basic technique: Inflate the canopy with the proper forward and upward arm movement. Perform a flight check, correct any malfunction or abort the takeoff if necessary, stabilize the canopy then progressively lighten your grip on the front risers while pushing them forward as you accelerate. Note: with some gliders you must release the front risers and apply the front brakes as you run. However, even in this case your arms are pulling on the risers. When you feel yourself being lifted off the ground, gently release the risers and deploy the brakes to flying position at shoulder height (see figure 61). On a very steep slope add brakes sooner, while a flat slope requires you to remain off brakes and accelerate hard. *CAUTION: Do not pull down on the front risers or the canopy will accelerate and fall in front of you (see figure 62).*

Also, do not let go of the front risers or pull on the brakes prematurely or the canopy will retard and never achieve flying speed. Here are the takeoff steps summarized:

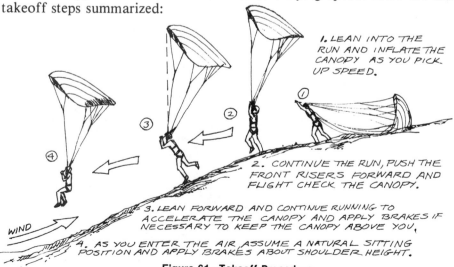

1. LEAN INTO THE RUN AND INFLATE THE CANOPY AS YOU PICK UP SPEED.

2. CONTINUE THE RUN, PUSH THE FRONT RISERS FORWARD AND FLIGHT CHECK THE CANOPY.

3. LEAN FORWARD AND CONTINUE RUNNING TO ACCELERATE THE CANOPY AND APPLY BRAKES IF NECESSARY TO KEEP THE CANOPY ABOVE YOU.

4. AS YOU ENTER THE AIR, ASSUME A NATURAL SITTING POSITION AND APPLY BRAKES ABOUT SHOULDER HEIGHT.

WIND

Figure 61 · Takeoff Procedure

Two pilots look up and back to flight check their canopies.

Also, do not let go of the front risers or pull on the brakes prematurely or the canopy will retard and never achieve flying speed. Here are the takeoff steps summarized:

> **Taking Off**
> 1. Inflate canopy with proper arm motion and a forward run.
> 2. Flight check and stabilize the canopy. Abort launch or clear the canopy if a problem exists.
> 3. Look in front of you and make the final takeoff decision.
> 4. Accelerate the canopy to takeoff speed by running and pushing the front risers with your hands or arms.
> 5. When your body gets lighter, move your hands from the risers to the flying position (brake about shoulder height). Continue running into the air. Don't jump!
> 6. Correct for speed and direction if necessary.
> *NOTE: For a advanced glider this procedure is altered somewhat and is explained in Chapter VIII.*

After flight checking, the pilot accelerates into the air.

Again the key to a good takeoff is smooth action and gentle transitions of hand positions and forces. Learn to take long strides to moon-walk into the air rather than perform frenetic stutter steps that are full of sound and fury and signify nothing. Soon your takeoffs will become automatic and you will quickly turn your attention to flying efficiently.

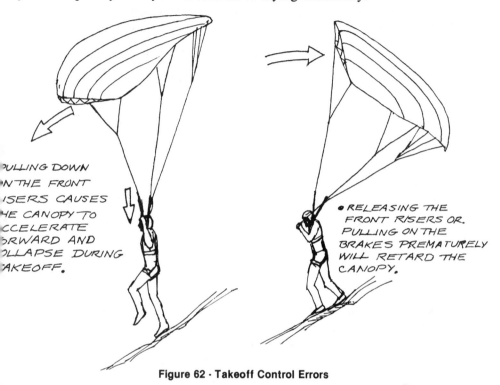

PULLING DOWN ON THE FRONT RISERS CAUSES THE CANOPY TO ACCELERATE FORWARD AND COLLAPSE DURING TAKEOFF.

• RELEASING THE FRONT RISERS OR PULLING ON THE BRAKES PREMATURELY WILL RETARD THE CANOPY.

Figure 62 · Takeoff Control Errors

In some schools your first takeoff may be at the end of a long rope. Tethering a paraglider is a safe method of getting into the air for the first time under the tutelage of a trained professional. Being tethered allows the instructor to control your height and stand by you while you perform correction controls. The lift-off technique is very simple, for you merely inflate the canopy then release the risers as the wind carries you upward. To come down you apply the brakes about half way or so to reduce the performance. In Chapter IX we review tethering.

Another matter you may experience in some schools is the instructor pulling you or pushing you to help you accelerate during takeoff. This is a useful procedure, especially in higher winds.

LEVEL FLIGHT—CORRECTIONS AND CONTROLS ——————

Immediately after you first ease into the air, you must think about heading straight to your intended landing area. To do this you must control the glider. We use the terms brakes, steering lines, control lines or toggles to mean the same thing for the toggles are connected to the control lines which are connected to the brakes that slow us when used simultaneously or steer us when used individually.

Let us look at straight flight first. Once you have committed to your take off, you must run continuously—no stopping and starting. When you are assured the canopy is fine you can look forward as you accelerate. Remain *off brakes* until you are definitely in the air for good, then apply a slight amount of brakes (about 25% or shoulder height). Do not slow down further until you are well clear of the terrain and stabilized in flight.

Try to relax in the harness and look down and forward at a focal point. Look forward to make sure you are going straight and look down to check your altitude. It is best to focus on your intended landing spot with careful checks to the side and down to monitor your progress and position.

Here are the controls for straight flying:

Flying Controls (Two Riser Systems)

1. Off Brakes to ¼ Brakes—this is where most canopies glide best and is the control position to use for gliding away from a hill and reaching furthest to a point. The hand position is from full up to about shoulder height, depending on the design (see figure 63). Consult the owner's manual for a particular glider to find the proper position.

Half Brakes—In this control position, most gliders will achieve their minimum sink rate. This position is found just below shoulder height normally and provides the slowest descent rate.

NOTE: Beginning pilots should not fly with controls below the shoulders until they log at least 20 flights

3. ¾ to Full Brakes—These positions are found at about the sternum (lower chest) and belly button position respectively. As the control toggles are moved to these positions, the glider gradually slows to the stall point.

4. Beyond Full Brakes (Stall)—As the controls are deployed several inches (8 cm or more) past the normal full brake position, stall is approached (see Chapter III). Maintaining this position will result in a stall that can be dangerous due to possible canopy collapse and a great loss of altitude. We cover stall practice in the next chapter. The stall brake position is also called the full stop position.

The various positions may be hard to learn at first, but remember that there is a continuum between each position and you will mostly learn to fly by feel and judgement. Besides, if you have trouble remembering the control positions, just get a T-shirt printed with lines on your chest at the cardinal points.

CAUTION: Always make all controls gradual for abrupt control actions make the canopy accelerate or decelerate. The effect of your controls depends not only on how much input you give, but also how fast you make this control.

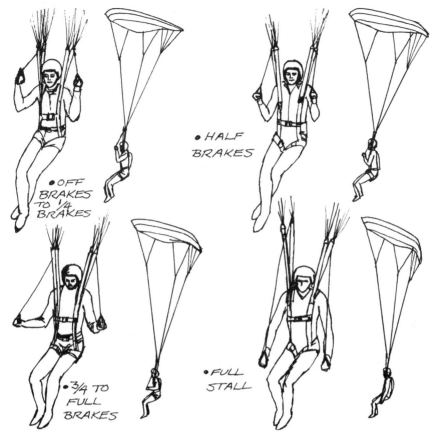

Figure 63 - Brake Positions

DIRECTION CONTROL

Direction corrections are an important part of your early training. In the following chapter we will learn how to turn, but for now we merely want to keep on the straight and narrow. By this time you probably know that pulling down on one toggle will unbalance the wing and turn the canopy. This is your correction control. You can make this control from any brake position except full brakes, for you do not want to pull one toggle to the stall position.

As a beginning pilot, however, you shouldn't be flying at slower speeds (with toggles below shoulders), so the control action is a smooth pull on the brake line of the advancing wing. For example, if the glider begins turning left, the pilot should immediately pull on the right toggle to deploy the right brake more and thus straighten out as shown in figure 64. During this correction procedure, be sure to keep the upper body relaxed so you can best judge the control input.

You should carefully time your release of the control to be neutral just before you are back on track. Otherwise you will overshoot. Don't release quickly if you see this happening, but perform an additional correction on the other side once your original correction is released. This time hold the control for less time.

Don't pull both toggles at once if you are trying to turn (a common beginner mistake), and don't pump the lines. All corrections should be smooth up and down controls with the top of the body relaxed. You can look at your hands if you wish to check yourself.

It is an ingrained human trait that we tend to go where we are looking. For this reason, it is important to look where we want to go, not what we want to avoid. It is amazing to discover how many pilots have flown directly into a lone tree in a large field because they were fixating on this one obstruction instead of where they needed to be flying. Remember, the eyes rule so here's...

The Rule of the Eyes
Look where you wish to go, not what you want to avoid for our vision often subconciously controls our body mechanics.

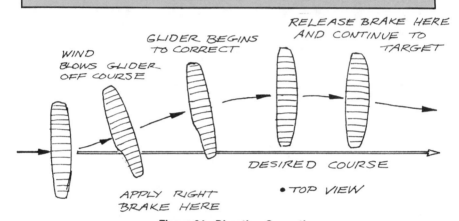

Figure 64 · Direction Correction

LANDINGS—THE ART OF ALIGHTING LIGHTLY

Alas, all good wings must come to a landing. If we are going to face this reality, we must learn to set down gently. In this chapter we are only concerned with straight forward uncomplicated landings. In the chapter following we will truly dissect the matter.

A good landing at the beginner level consists of approaching straight into the wind and touching down lightly with few, if any, steps. There are three phases to a good landing:

Phase 1—As you approach the ground, increase your airspeed to overcome the effects of turbulence and wind gradient as well as allow for a flatter glide when you slow in the next phase. This speed is achieved by coming off both brakes (arms up). At about 40 feet (12m) up, ease out of the harness by standing up to prepare to brake your descent and run.

Phase 2—At approximately 15 feet (4.5 m) above the ground, apply both brakes smoothly to just below the shoulders (half brakes). This braking action allows you to achieve a flatter glide by paying off speed for height. This landing phase is called the *roundout*.

Phase 3—When your feet are about six feet (2 m) off the ground, slow to touch down gently by pulling the brake controls down and through the axis of the body to full stop position at the knees as shown in figure 65. The final braking should be completed when the feet are 2 feet (.6 m) off the ground. This phase is called the *flare*. If your timing is correct, your sink rate and your forward speed should be zero just as you touch down.

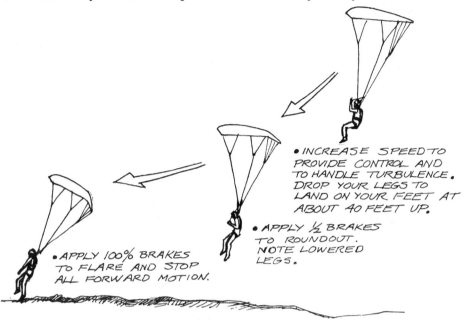

• INCREASE SPEED TO PROVIDE CONTROL AND TO HANDLE TURBULENCE. DROP YOUR LEGS TO LAND ON YOUR FEET AT ABOUT 40 FEET UP.

• APPLY ½ BRAKES TO ROUNDOUT. NOTE LOWERED LEGS.

• APPLY 100% BRAKES TO FLARE AND STOP ALL FORWARD MOTION.

Figure 65 · Landing Sequence

During this landing process you should be concentrating on the ground in front of you (don't look straight down until the final touch down or you will not have good spatial judgement) where you intend to land. You should have been studying the ground from an altitude of 75 to 100 feet (23 to 30 m) to note wind direction and the lay of the land where you will come down. If a wind shift surprises you or you get turned off course, it is better to land crosswind than to attempt low level turns. As a beginning pilot you should be landing in light winds, of course. Remember your goal is a long, straight final into the wind.

If perchance you flare (pull the brakes to full stop) too soon, the canopy will move behind you and you will be pulled immediately back. If you come off the brakes the canopy may surge ahead of you and plunge you to the ground. If you find yourself flaring too soon, stop your action immediately then follow through with brakes to the knees at the appropriate time. In general, the glider will not respond to a second pump if you come off the brakes so it is best to hold your position if you begin to flare prematurely. Of course, the flare action is a stall, so flaring too high, too vigorously can be dangerous.

If you flare too low you will come in harder than normal. However, in most cases you will be able to run out your landing. Keep your landing gear ready to spring to action in this case (for hard landings we will teach a landing roll later).

The secret to a good landing is to relax so that you can use your practic-

81

ed judgement. Of course, on your first few flights you don't have much practice, but your instructor will assist you on your flare timing and soon you will find it easy, for the landing approach is slow. Be cautious of developing a dependence on your instructor's landing commands, for you must soon learn to make such decisions on your own.

> **Landing Procedures**
> 1. Align yourself to head directly into the wind from 75 to 100 feet (23 to 30 m).
> 2. Make last small direction corrections no lower than 20 feet (6 m). Turns below 75 feet should be less than 15°.
> 3. Maintain good airspeed below 50 feet (15 m) by coming off brakes.
> 4. Stand up in the harness at about 40 feet (12 m).
> 5. At about 15 feet (4.5 m) apply half brakes (shoulder height) smoothly to slow down and roundout.
> 6. At about 6 feet (2 m) apply full stop brakes to flare and touch down with finesse and grace.

A pilot pulls brakes full on to flare for landing.

GRADUAL PROGRESSION

After you have landed the first few times, think about what you felt. Chances are you were so excited the flight memories were vague. That's normal and the clear thinking will come later after you begin to relax.

Practice these elementary flights over and over again until you feel confident and calm at the initial learning altitude, then move up the hill in increments of 10 or 20 feet (3 to 6 m). Your instructor will pace you here. Remember, often the pilot that progresses slowly at first turns out to be the one that excels later due to his or her sound grounding in the basic skills from which all advanced skills develop.

TOTING AND STOWING

After your flight you must take your paraglider back to the staging area and more importantly, clear it from the landing area lest it disturb incoming traffic. To do this, collapse the canopy in the normal manner then hold the connecting links and gather the lines in hand over hand toward the canopy. Don't drag the canopy toward you, but walk toward it, then sling it over your shoulder for carrying (see figure 66). Keep the canopy on your downwind shoulder or it will blow over your head, and make sure it doesn't drag the ground as you walk. Watch out for nasty bushes that love to snag canopies.

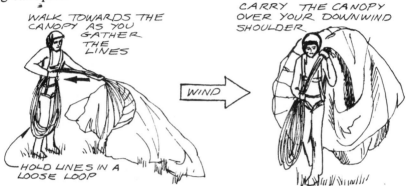

Figure 66 · Carrying Off The Field

At the end of the day you must stow the canopy in it's pack. Here are the simple steps to the most popular and quickest packing method:

1. As shown in figure 67, lay the canopy on its back (the same as during takeoff), then put the harness and lines in the center of the canopy as neatly as possible.

Figure 67 · Placing Harness on Canopy For Packing

2. Now begin at either end and fold the canopy like an accordian in toward the center as shown in figure 68. This is much easier with two people. If you are alone, you can roll the canopy cell by cell. However, rolling the canopy has a greater tendency to entangle lines since they twist around each other during the rolling process. Be sure to remove all debris and grass as you fold the canopy. Smooth each fold as you proceed.

3. Finally, fold the two sides together over the harness then fold the entire package lengthwise as necessary to fit in the pack as shown in figure 69. Push the air of the canopy as you make the final folds for the smallest possible package.

You may alternately choose to keep the lines out of the canopy and

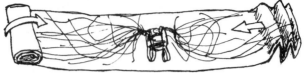

ROLL THE CANOPY FROM EACH END OR ACCORDIAN FOLD IT.

PUSH AIR OUT OF THE FOLDS AS YOU GO.

Figure 68 · Initial Folding of the Canopy

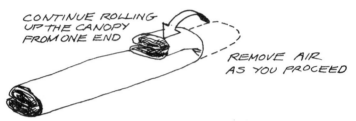

CONTINUE ROLLING UP THE CANOPY FROM ONE END

REMOVE AIR AS YOU PROCEED

Figure 69 · Final Folding of the Canopy

Folding a modern paraglider.

Carrying off the field.

braid or chain-link them separately in order to prevent entanglement. Chain-linking the lines is a slick trick that usually takes a few tries to master, but the learning is fun. Practice it with friends and see how many parties you get invited to. Figure 70(a-d) illustrates the process. Starting at the canopy, loop the lines over your hand then slide the hand through to grasp the lines and pull them through the previous loop. The finished product should appear as in figure 70e.

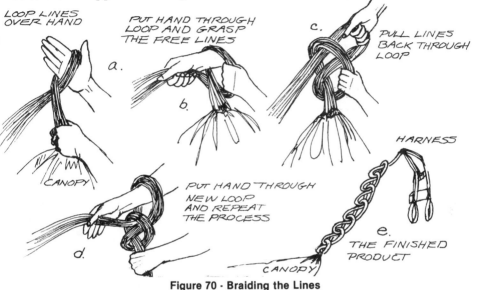

Figure 70 · Braiding the Lines

As you fold your canopy, brush off the weeds, leaves and grass from the surface. These small items can abraid your canopy during storage. Don't sit on your packed glider for this very reason. When you operate in areas with high weeds, small bits may enter into the cells. They are hard to remove because static electricity makes them stick. Try starting at the trailing edge and shaking them to the front as you lift the canopy. In any case, when you get home you can clean the inside of the canopy with a long-hosed vacuum cleaner.

Once your canopy is folded, store the entire package—harness, lines and canopy—in the pack and you have ended another fine day (almost).

AT THE END OF THE DAY

While you are dreaming of the rapturous heights you have achieved, don't forget that you have a responsibility to yourself to keep a log book of your progress. This log book will become very useful to you as you continue in the sport for you will be able to present it to those inquiring about your experience as well as have an impressive document for your own later recollections.

Two other important reasons justify log books. First, you can use them to spot trends or trouble areas. Many pilots have detected the beginning of a bad flying habit through their log book. Secondly, your instructor can sign your log book as he or she witnesses you perform tasks required for various classifications and special skills of the APA rating system (see Appendix I).

A log book can be simply a ruled notebook, or you can purchase one designed specifically for sport aviation. An example of a log book appears in figure 71. Don't neglect to fill it out and you'll have a personal flying history.

DATE	FLIGHT DESCRIPTION	LOCATION	CONDITIONS	GLIDER	WITNESS
3/8/91	TOOK OFF IN LIGHT AIR. GAINED 300 FT. SOARED 45 MIN.	MAGIC MT., KANSAS	WINDS 8-10 SMOOTH, WARM	PARA-MAGIC	Otto Lilienthal
4/9/91	TOOK 3 SLED RIDES IN LIGHT AIR GOOD LANDINGS!	MOUNT TOWLINE, IOWA	WINDS 0-3 STABLE	PARA-MAGIC	Wilbur Wright

Figure 71 · Log Book Example

SUMMARY

You have learned to fly! While daydreaming in your busy day, try to review your flights. What did you accomplish? What can you improve? Once you get to the point where you are launching, flying smoothly and landing consistently, you have mastered the difficult part. The rest is gravy.

If you experienced fear, don't worry. This is a natural reaction which you will overcome if you stay at one level until confidence builds. Watch the birds: a fledgling also has trouble learning to fly at times. Soon you will be joining these birds high aloft.

The following set of safety rules will serve you well throughout your flying experience:

Safety Rules
1. Never fly alone.
2. Never fly when overly tired.
3. Never fly under the influence of drugs (including alcohol).
4. Always wear a helmet.
5. Always take off and land into the wind.
6. Deflate your canopy immediately after landing.
7. Never add more than one new thing at a time (new glider, new site, etc).
8. The wind complicates all flying—the stronger the wind, the greater the complications.
9. Judgement takes the longest time to acquire of any aspect in aviation.
10. Always fly one step below your limits.

If you have learned your lessons well and follow these safety rules, you should be able to pass the Beginner Rating Requirements (see Appendix I).

CHAPTER VI

At Home In The Air
Novice Skills

Just south of Salt Lake City in Utah there is a popular flying site frequented by paraglider, hang glider and the occasional ultralight pilot. This site is in full view of a maximum security prison, and one can't help but ponder the irony of observing mankind in his most free state in such proximity to mankind in irons. Certainly the prisoners can see the colorful wings soaring high over their heads. They can't be blamed for ruing the contrast to their fate.

But there is another prison in full view of the happy pilots. It is I-15, the expressway that heads south to Las Vegas. Here the prisoners ride in enclosed comfort, but they are equally bound by the strictures of their vision, society and lifestyle. They ride along ignorant of the freedom that is available to them. Perhaps theirs is the greatest error, for when they are through with a life of building empires, will they truly have lived their life to its fullest extent?

You will occasionally encounter spectators who smugly announce "You've got to be crazy to fly those things." To them the only appropriate reply is "Actually, the crazy ones are those who witness the final realization of humanity's dreams of pure flight and don't have the will to participate." Smile when you say this.

You have chosen to taste the freedom. But with this freedom comes a responsibility to fly safely and represent the sport in a reasonable manner. No one will benefit if accidents occur, least of all the perpetrating pilot. To fly safely you must develop judgement. You do this by carefully building your experience and analyzing your decisions. The purpose of judgement is to help you define the limits of safety.

In this chapter we learn to explore the sky within the bounds of these limits. We will give you guidelines in all facets of flight that you will use to hone your judgement. Remember the old adage:

> *"A superior pilot uses his superior judgement to avoid using his superior skills."*

By the end of this chapter you should have acquired the necessary skills to pass the APA Noice Rating. However, your judgement may still require work. Don't rush matters. Paragliding is fun at all levels and it is only ego that induces us to fly with the aces before we are ready. Remember, flying is 25% skill and 75% judgement. Developing this judgement takes time. The ultimate exercise of judgement may be stated:

> *When in doubt, do not fly.*

FLIGHT PLANS

Every flight should begin with a flight plan. At the beginning stages this plan should be complete, yet simple, for your flights should be simple. Plan what conditions you will launch in, what direction you will head, what altitude you will enter landing mode (mentally and physically). What direction and where you will land. Later you will add complexities such as what varied ground path you will follow and where you will observe for other traffic. Much later you may include areas to explore for lift. Finally, your plan may become merely a direction to turn after launch and an altitude to head out for landing as well as areas to avoid due to sink or turbulence.

You should make your flight plan at takeoff just before launching. In the beginning stages it helps to discuss your plan with your instructor. In fact, for the first few flights your instructor will give you your flight plan.

Once your plan is made, mentally file it away and concentrate on launching. As soon as you are airborne, recall and follow your flight plan with a constant review to alter it if new influences appear. Remember, the air is a changing fluid and you never have all the information about its future state at your disposal. Be flexible enough to vary your flight plan as unexpected conditions appear. The very best flight plans are those with alternative paths to follow to handle all contingencies.

TAKEOFF PERMUTATIONS

In the last chapter we discussed the basics of taking off in ideal conditions. Here we extend our experience to handle reality: often less than perfect wind and terrain. Every day is unique , but we can discuss general conditions.

Before we begin with the various techniques, we should mention the mental preparedness necessary to handle less than perfect conditions at launch. First, you should be confident of your own ability to safely complete the task at hand. If not, wait until conditions improve or pack up and return another day. Secondly, don't be pressured into hurrying your launch by other pilots equally anxious to get off the hill (if necessary, step aside and let them go first). Finally, when you do judge conditions to be safe for you, make the decision to go and progress without hesitation for a smooth, continuous, successful launch. Tentative controls or runs are not compatible with more difficult launch situations.

CALM OR LIGHT WIND ASSISTED TAKEOFF

The takeoff procedures in Chapter V were those for calm and light winds with assistance. Reread these to refresh your familiarity with them if necessary. The only thing to add here is that if you have only one assistant he or she should stand in the middle of the canopy with the canopy arched as shown in figure 72. This arching allows the canopy to inflate progressively from the center outward. Also, with a very large canopy a third assistant may be used in this center position with the canopy almost straight.

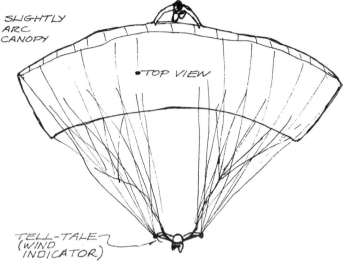

Figure 72 · Light Wind Assisted Takeoff

CALM OR LIGHT WIND UNASSISTED TAKEOFF

If you are by yourself in no wind, you essentially follow the same control motions as before, but you prepare the canopy differently. Begin with the canopy gathered into a horseshoe shape as shown in figure 73. Here the first three cells per side have been gathered in completely at the trailing edge. This allows the canopy to "scoop" the air better as you accelerate and it inflates progressively.

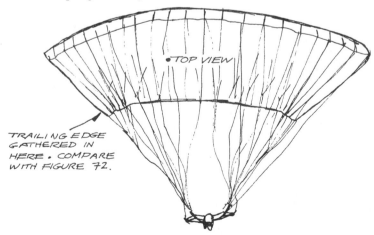

Figure 73 · Light Wind Unassisted Takeoff

When you start to run, both arms must pull *together* and you must be very sure to start in the middle of the canopy (as always). You must create a wind by running with a smooth motion. You may have to hold on to the front risers a little longer in this case to prevent the canopy from tilting back. The key to a good calm wind launch is fluid motion and continuous running. Do not stop until you are in the air.

PRO-TIP: At the point where you just come off the ground, applying a slight amount of brakes will help lift off. Using brakes too soon will cause drag that prevents lift off.

WINDY ASSISTED TAKEOFF

In these conditions the ground crew holds the trailing edge of the canopy tightly to the ground and grasps the leading edge with their rearward hand as explained in Chapter V. An additional assistant holds you by the harness for you may be pulled backwards by the force of the wind when the canopy is rising behind you (see figure 74). Once it is over your head you can control in a normal manner for the rearward pull is reduced. This method should only be used in winds of 10 mph (16 km/h) or less. Above this the rearward pull is too great and the canopy should be gathered to reduce the rearward force (see below).

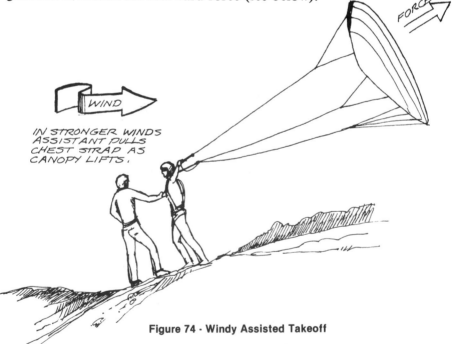

IN STRONGER WINDS ASSISTANT PULLS CHEST STRAP AS CANOPY LIFTS.

WIND

FORCE

Figure 74 - Windy Assisted Takeoff

The assistants on the canopy should lift the leading edge about one foot when you are ready while holding the trailing edge taut and down. This allows the canopy to straighten and reduces the chance of malfunctions. On your command they lift as usual while letting go of the trailing edge. It is extremely important that they not lift the trailing edge.

In winds above 10 mph you can start by laying your canopy out "gathered". This involves laying it on its back and unfolding only the center section. Some pilots who roll their canopies just unroll the two sides enough to expose the center cells. The idea is to create a gradual inflation which reduces the force on you, the pilot. The danger of a high wind inflation is being pulled backwards by the canopy during inflation as shown in the figure (once it is above you the problem goes away unless you drop the canopy back by applying both brakes too much).

When a canopy inflates from the gathered position, it unrolls in the air and there is a good chance a line entanglement will occur. It is important to check the lines carefully in this case. Plucking a line like a guitar string can often remove entanglements. This action may also remove small sticks and other debris as well. In any case, we recommend reverse launches (see below) highly in any unassisted windy launch.

Skip Beland gets assistance from John Bouchard in soaring winds.

In windy conditions you should stay on the front risers until the canopy is over your head. Then move smoothly to control with the toggles to stabilize the canopy. Use the brakes individually to keep the canopy from oscillating and use a combination of the brakes and front risers to position the canopy forward and back. This technique should be practiced carefully with your instructor holding your harness. It will be reviewed after the next two sections.

The assistant on your harness should not let go until you yell CLEAR! He or she should flight check your canopy for you and move with you if necessary to affect a takeoff. Perform your normal controls as you fly away from the hill.

WINDY UNASSISTED TAKEOFF

This is the most tricky situation, but it is easily mastered with practice. To begin, you lay the canopy out in a very tight horsehoe and weight the inside corners as shown in figure 75. Note that the cells aren't gathered as before, but the whole canopy is curved. The weight should be a smooth rock or a sand bag weighing about 3 or 4 lbs (1.5 to 2 kg). The idea is for the canopy to pull out from under this weight as you begin takeoff, so don't use a boulder and don't place it too far onto the canopy. All you are trying to do is to keep the wind from blowing the canopy out of position. Some pilots use small sticks stuck through the parking tabs and into the ground in windy conditions, but this practice can result in a stick going for a ride with you. You can also lay the canopy flat as normal and place several rocks along the trailing edge.

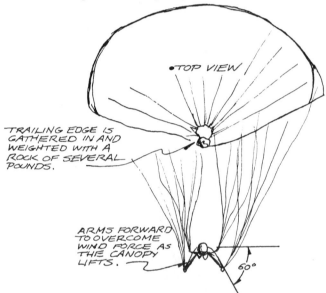

Figure 75 - Unassisted Windy Takeoff

A pilot inflates in higher winds.

92

Once you are in your harness in front of the canopy, tease the front risers with your arms stretched at a 30° angle as shown in the figure to get the canopy filled across the back. Now move forward while moving your hands clear up over your head (maintain the 30° angle) until the canopy is above you. Lean into your run and gain momentum before the canopy drags you back.

Again you have to correct the canopy position with the brakes and the front risers, but see below.

REVERSE INFLATION

Now we come to an important technique recommended for all windy launches. This is performing a reverse inflation and flight check. To do this, prepare yourself in the harness in the normal manner with the rear risers drooped over your arms and the front risers in your hands but hands off the brake toggles. Now turn around bringing the risers on the outside of your turn over your head so they are all lying in front of you (you are now facing the canopy) with a half twist.

With your arms in front of you at a 30° angle, tease the canopy by jiggling the lines to begin the inflation evenly across the back of the canopy, then lift your stretched out arms clearly up over your head to inflate the canopy as you back up (see figure 76).

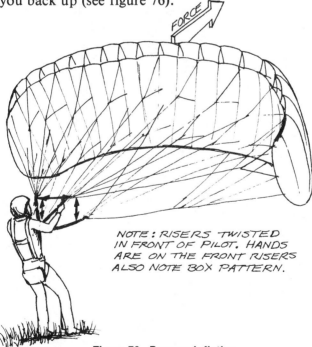

FORCE

NOTE: RISERS TWISTED IN FRONT OF PILOT. HANDS ARE ON THE FRONT RISERS ALSO NOTE BOX PATTERN.

Figure 76 · Reverse Inflation

Once the canopy is over your head, the risers will be crossed but the inflation will be normal. Stabilize the canopy using the front and rear risers. Check the forward movement of the canopy with the rear risers—don't let it sail past you. If the canopy gets tilted to one side, pull the rear riser on the high side, then move the other hand to the front riser on this side to

A reverse inflation—note crossed risers.

keep the canopy up over your head with a little pull. Figure 76 indicates how your hands move in a box pattern from the rear and front riser on one side to the front and rear riser on the other. Think of it as a simple box dance step. *Do not* reach inside the risers and *do not* cross your arms.

Common errors when performing a reverse inflation other than reaching inside the "box" are over controlling and turning of the canopy away from the wind. Only practice will overcome these problems. Note: this technique (reverse inflation) is also advised when you have assistance in which case your assistant holds the back of your harness while you flight check the canopy or practice your controls. Also, this is a good time to inspect your brake adjustment as you can readily, see the rear of the canopy. We'll make mention here that the reverse position is useful for climbing hills in great moonwalk steps with the canopy acting like a spinaker to pull you uphill (see Chapter IX).

The main purpose of reverse inflation is to help you through the vulnerable period when your canopy begins to inflate and threatens to drag you backwards. There are times, however, when a gust or miscalculation of the wind's strength may overcome you. In this case you must be able to quickly "kill the sail" to prevent being dragged along the ground. The reverse launch position is the best position to do this effectivily.

To "kill the sail" or deflate in an emergency, pull on both rear risers as hard as possible while running toward the canopy. The canopy will stall and fall back immediately. Remember, in a strong wind you may be lifted unexpectedly so be securely strapped in with your helmet in place whenever you attempt a reverse inflation.

To take off when you have turned backwards, you must have the canopy steady or it will be out of position by the time you turn around. It must be flying clearly above your head. Make your turn, steady the canopy, then grab the brake toggles, then push forward on the front risers, run down the hill then return to the control position once you have launched. If you need to abort the takeoff at any point, remember all you have to do is pull both brakes together fully and the canopy will drop. Remember, at some point the wind may be too strong to self launch safely. In this case you may consider moving down the hill to lesser winds.

CROSSWIND TAKEOFFS

We acknowledged before that the wind is not always going to be perfectly up the slope. We also set a limit of 30° for the wind to be off the straight-in direction for our current level of flying. Furthermore, this crosswind should be limited to 12 mph (20 km/h).

The technique for handling such a crossing wind is to lay out the glider facing the wind direction (across the hill the necessary amount as in figure 77), then perform a normal inflation facing the wind. Once the canopy moves over your head, perform a flight check, stabilize the canopy then quickly move down the hill to get the canopy flying. Your canopy will begin by being angled to the hill which automatically sets up a crab angle, but you will probably have to correct this somewhat since your flying speed will be greater than the wind speed. Make these corrections smoothly as soon as you get in the air and establish your flight path.

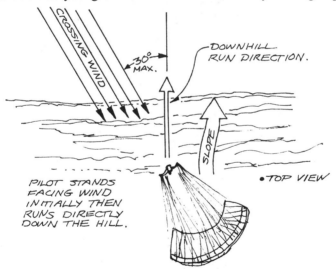

Figure 77 · Crosswind Takeoff Technique

USING THE RISERS IN FLIGHT

As we mentioned in Chapter V, pulling down on the risers directly changes the angle of attack of the canopy. Pulling the front risers lowers the angle of attack and pulling the rear risers raises it. The canopy will fly faster and slower respectively (see figure 78).

When you are flight checking the canopy in wind, you may steer at the same time you are pulling on the risers by pulling one riser more than the other. To correct fore and aft oscillations, use the front risers and brakes (not the rear risers). You have to be nimble and precise to stop the oscillations without overcontrolling, possibly moving from risers to brakes to risers! If you wait too long to make corrections, the canopy may go past the neutral point and have to be recorrected. Anticipate the reactions.

In flight, pulling down on the front risers will effectively increase your flying speed. However, this may be at the expense of glide ratio and should be used only to penetrate a higher wind or in an emergency to lose altitude quickly. Experiment with this for the first time with plenty of ground clearance. Be sure to make such controls smoothly. Do not abruptly release the front risers or the glider may stall dynamically. Also, with some canopies, pulling down the front risers excessively can deflate the front of the canopy resulting in a rapid loss of altitude. Releasing the risers and applying brakes is the recovery procedure here.

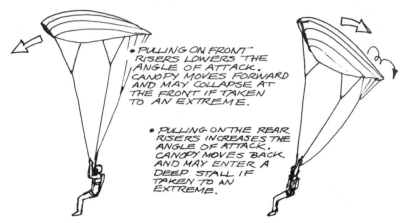

• PULLING ON FRONT RISERS LOWERS THE ANGLE OF ATTACK. CANOPY MOVES FORWARD AND MAY COLLAPSE AT THE FRONT IF TAKEN TO AN EXTREME.

• PULLING ON THE REAR RISERS INCREASES THE ANGLE OF ATTACK. CANOPY MOVES BACK AND MAY ENTER A DEEP STALL IF TAKEN TO AN EXTREME.

Figure 78 · Pulling on Risers

Pulling both the rear risers will slow you and should be done with caution for you can deep stall the wing as you raise its angle of attack. Some canopies are equipped with trim tabs on the rear risers which allow you to pull them down and hold the wing at a new (higher) angle of attack. See the section on deep stalls in this chapter concerning trim tabs.

Flying with the rear risers is an important skill that should be well practiced by the time a pilot is flying high regularly. This is an emergency procedure necessary if one or both brakes become non-functional by virtue of a toggle coming off or a brake line looped around itself at the grommet (the latter is the most frequent occurence resulting from a poor preflight). If you are familiar with using the rear risers, such an event need not be a major emergency for you can calmly pilot away from the hill and free the brake once you have plenty of clearance.

Almost all maneuvers that can be performed with the brakes can be performed with the rear risers, including landing, for pulling the rear risers warps the canopy similar to brake deployment. If only one brake is out of commission, do all the piloting with both rear risers, rather than one brake and one riser, in order to produce symmetrical turns.

For canopies trimmed faster than best glide, pulling the rear risers will improve the glide ratio more efficiently than will brakes. For gliders trimmed hands-off for best glide, pulling the rear risers has no real advantage.

Again we remind you to use smooth control movements.

CAUTION: Pulling the risers in flight is dangerous at the limits and should be initially tried only with ample altitude (at least 300 feet).

FLYING IN WIND

As we have learned, wind is a complicating factor in aviation (except perhaps when it assists our foot-launched takeoffs). The forces of the wind increases with the square of the velocity, so increased wind can serve to make our job of control more critical. In general, in wind our controls must be more precise and immediate. *The maximum recommended (smooth) wind for a Novice pilot is 12 mph (19 km/h).*

Flying in wind results in varying ground speeds and tracks. In wind we are like a boat in a river, moving with the current. If we head upwind (up current) the wind slows our progress with respect to the ground. If we head downwind, the wind speeds our progress and if we head crosswind we fly at an angle to our heading just as a boat heading directly across a river moves partially sideways.

In figure 79 we see the effects of flying in a head or tail wind. The wind speed is always added (vectorally) to our airspeed to give us groundspeed.

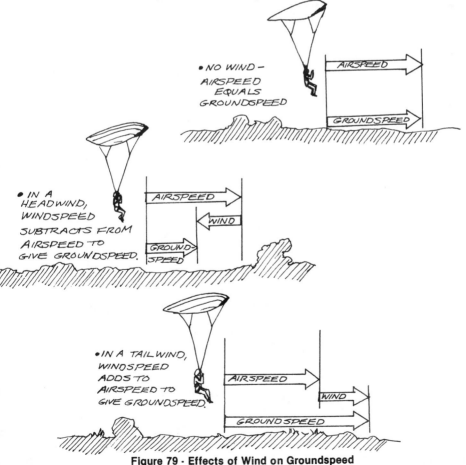

Figure 79 · Effects of Wind on Groundspeed

97

Whether you are flying upwind or downwind your flight controls are the same. Your glider moves along in the fluid (air) and can feel no difference no matter which direction it is flying with respect to the wind. The same is true of an upwind and downwind turn—no difference above the effects of wind gradient.

The only actual difference in all these maneuvers in wind is your motion with respect to the ground and your perception. Of course, if you turn downwind very close to the ground and land with a tailwind, you'll feel physics in action, but the glider perceives no difference.

The preceding matter can again be illustrated by invoking nautical images if we take a boat far at sea in a strong ocean current. Out of sight of land the passengers can detect no difference when moving up current or down current, nor can they feel a difference in a turn into the current or away from the current direction. To them the fluid is stationary and so it is to your glider in moving air (as long as the air is not turbulent of course).

CRABBING TECHNIQUES

When the wind is from one side it pushes us from our intended path as shown in figure 80a. We may eventually arrive at our intended goal by keeping our heading pointed at this goal (80b), but this is a very inefficient way to fly. Far better is to turn our canopy the amount required to offset the wind-drift effect and move directly towards our goal (80c). This technique is called crabbing because we move partially sideways like a crab. In this case your ground track does not follow your heading (the direction you are pointed).

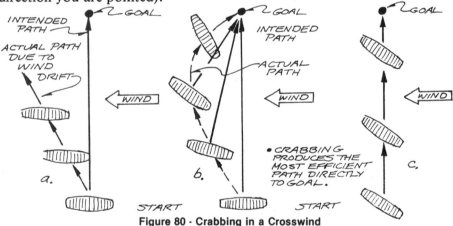

Figure 80 · Crabbing in a Crosswind

To learn crabbing technique you don't have to calculate angles and all that nasty trigonometric stuff, you simply look at your desired goal and turn into the wind until you are moving directly to it. It helps to lay out an imaginary ground track along the ground below you as check points. If you find yourself drifting downwind too much, turn a bit more into the wind and vice versa if you drift upwind.

FLYING IN TURBULENCE—CANOPY COLLAPSE

We have already identified turbulence as random or organized swirls in

Chapter IV. What effect does this have on our flying? The standard aircraft problem with all but extreme turbulence is control. However, with a paraglider, the great pendulum stability and the powerful turn controls render this classic problem essentially nil. The real problem here is canopy collapse.

In stronger winds and in thermals we should expect turbulence. Also, flying behind another aircraft will put us in the path of their wing tip vortices. This should be avoided assiduously for wing vortices are perfectly formed to collapse a canopy. Hang gliders and other paragliders are likely to be the main type of aircraft you encounter. All these pilots should be informed of their effect on paraglider wings.

To reduce the chance of a canopy collapse, do not fly too fast, for forces of the moving air increase with airspeed. Likewise, don't fly too slowly or the random air movement may stall you. The best speed to fly in turbulence with a two riser system is with brakes from 50% to 70% deployed (toggles between shoulders and lower chest). This position keeps the canopy well inflated. Also, you should be aware that lighter wing loadings increase your susceptibility to turbulence due to your lower airspeed with respect to the gust velocity. Smaller canopies flown at a moderate speed seem to be the best set-up for handling turbulence.

In turbulence and other threatening situations check the canopy frequently to detect an incipient collapse. If you get a feeling something is strange, your first reaction should be to check the canopy. Eventually you will detect a problem immediately by learning to feel a change in brake and harness forces. Usual effects of turbulence include some weightlessness, swinging in the harness and a loss in performance.

In the event of a canopy collapse, don't panic. Remember, your canopy is a ram air device and as long as there is air moving it will want to inflate. You can help this re-inflation by quickly giving a pump or two on *both* brakes (even if only one side collapses). Pull the toggles to chest level, release them then return to chest level (see figure 81). You can repeat this procedure if the first attempt is not successful.

If the canopy turns which is usually the case if one side collapses, pull on the outside brake line to straighten it so you do not turn steeply. Focus on

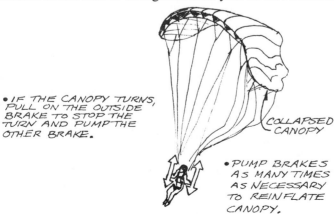

•IF THE CANOPY TURNS, PULL ON THE OUTSIDE BRAKE TO STOP THE TURN AND PUMP THE OTHER BRAKE.

COLLAPSED CANOPY

•PUMP BRAKES AS MANY TIMES AS NECESSARY TO REINFLATE CANOPY.

Figure 81 · Canopy Collapse

a bearing and try to keep the glider flying straight and level. While you are making this control, pump the inside brake to effect reinflation. Remember, the deflation is only temporary, but you will lose altitude. For this reason, be alert to quickly remedy any canopy collapse when turbulence appears. Watching your canopy can help you get a jump on an incipient collapse. Encountering sudden sink can feel like a collapsed canopy, so vigilance and a quick check of the canopy can keep you well on top of matters.

When your canopy recovers you will hear a thump and feel a tug on your harness. Continually check the canopy to make sure it is in proper shape. Remember the old ounce and pound adage; prevent canopy collapse best by avoiding the most turbulent part of the day (usually between 12:00 and 3:00 pm) and strong winds. Then you won't have to affect the above outlined cure.

FLYING AT ALTITUDE

With more altitude you will be encountering more varied conditions. Reread Chapter IV to understand the nuances of the restless air. You will begin to find lift and sink on your flights from higher hills. Generally, this air motion is benign and only is a problem if midday thermals are virulent. Maintain your best turbulence control speed when such conditions threaten (see Chapter VIII for thermal flying techniques). Also, as a general rule of thumb you should speed up a bit in sinking air to pass through it more quickly and thus minimize your altitude loss.

Since the wind increases as we rise above the surface, do we reach an unlimited velocity? The answer is simply no. Generally, the wind reaches a maximum velocity caused by the pressure systems at 1500 to 3000 ft (500 to 900 m). The lower number corresponds to smooth surfaces and the upper number to rough surfaces.

In areas where the jet stream (strong high altitude wind) exists, the wind can continue to increase with altitude, but a paraglider would be hard put to come anywhere near the jet stream altitudes. Generally, if you take off in winds that are safe and allow leeway for gradient effects (say 5 to 10 mph), you should not encounter dangerous high winds, even if you gain great height in lift. Any overly vigorous wind aloft will usually make itself felt at the surface and can be judged to be safe or not safe before you take off.

One final point to understand concerning the variation of wind with altitude, is that the wind most often turns counterclockwise as we gain height. Typically the wind turns to the right about 45° from ground level to 3000 ft (900 m). However, the turn direction and amount can vary significantly from this norm due to local effects and upper air disturbances. The reasons for this are beyond the scope of this book (see *Flying Conditions*), but all pilots should be aware of the possibilities for wind direction changes and leave ample safety margins in their flying.

As you first fly higher you may experience what is called the dive syndrome. When you are close to the ground you see the ground objects moving by quickly. When you are high for the first time, everything seems to crawl. Your eyes send a suble message to the brain that reads "Hey, what do those hands want to do, stall and cause our hard-working heart to go on strike?" The brain responds in kind by causing the hands to move to dive speed. Fortunately with a paraglider this is not much of a problem but the beginner pilot is cautioned to *stay off* the front risers during their early high altitude experience. Of course these early high flights should be made in light winds. Remember to fly with airspeed not groundspeed.

ALTITUDE AND GLIDE JUDGEMENT

The matter of altitude judgement and glide path judgement should be mentioned. Your brain is not well prepared to judge altitude by looking directly at the ground. You have little background to relate to. Learn to judge altitude by judging your angle up from a known position. As we shall see, this is useful when setting up landing approaches.

You can tell if you have enough altitude to clear an obstruction (building, power line, hill or trees) by looking at the ground behind the obstruction. If you continously see more ground just behind the obstruction you will clear it. If you see less ground, forget it, you're not going to make it and should choose another landing area. This is illustrated in figure 82a.

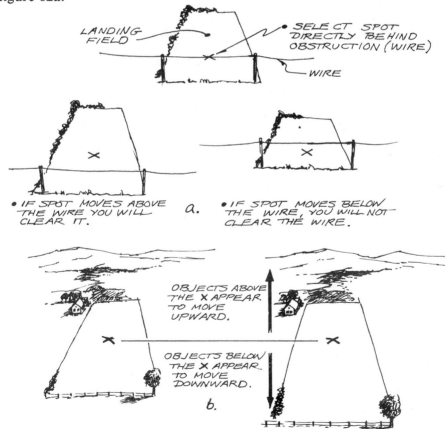

Figure 82 · Glide Path Judgement

101

One trick to use is to place your spread hand above your knee. A line from your eye through the top of your hand to the ground in front of you will be your normal glide path. Of course, this measurement varies with the harness type, your leg lengths, your hand size and your glider performance. Start with this rule of thumb then alter it according to your situation by carrying out a few trials.

Another technique allows you to determine about where you are going to land. Any point in front of you beyond your flight path will appear to rise in your vision as the angle to it increases upward (see figure 82b). Any point which you can pass in your glide will appear to drop in your vision as the angle increases downward. The point to which you are gliding will remain stationary and this method is aptly named the stationary point method.

Glide Judgement

•If you are going to clear an object, more ground will appear behind the object.

•If your glide is not adequate to clear an object, ground will disappear behind the object.

•Any point beyond your glide path will appear to rise as you progress.

•Any point below your glide path will appear to sink.

•The point you will reach will remain stationary in your viewpoint.

Once you are comfortable at altitude, it's time to practice various important controls. Perform these practices methodically and record your experience in your trusty log book. Here's what to do. Try flying hands off the brakes and feel the glider's natural trim speed. Next try steering with the rear risers, then the front risers. Follow this by changing angle of attack with the risers (see **Using the Risers**). Next, experience a number of mild stalls and recoveries, but not before reading the next section...

STALL PRACTICE

We know from our study that a stall occurs when we get the angle of attack too high. This also occurs at too slow an airspeed. We practice stalls so that we recognize their signs, results and recovery techniques in the case of an inadvertent stall.

Here's the method. First, be warned that a severe stall or dynamic stall is dangerous. In this case much more altitude is lost as the glider falls trying to regain airspeed. We discuss deep stalls at the end of this chapter. Figure 83 illustrates a dynamic stall. Here the pilot has either pulled the brakes too fast or entered the stall with too much speed or both. As the angle of attack rises the canopy retards, swinging the pilot forward due to inertia which further increases the angle of attack. When the wing finally stalls it is at a much higher *attitude* than with a normal stall as shown in the figure.

To practice a safe stall, first obtain plenty of ground clearance. Five hundred feet (150 m) is a minimum, although 1000 feet (300 m) is ideal. Now head into the wind and slow the glider down to full brake position. Let the airspeed stabilize for a few seconds, then *gradually* apply more brakes until you feel the canopy burble and a sudden drop or increase in sink rate. This is the stall point and you should immediately return your hands to shoulder height (½ brake) and the canopy will recover. Don't go to off brake position or the canopy will accelerate in front of you. Watch the canopy as you stall to see the characteristic deformation of the canopy into a beginning horseshoe shape. This is another sign of a stall.

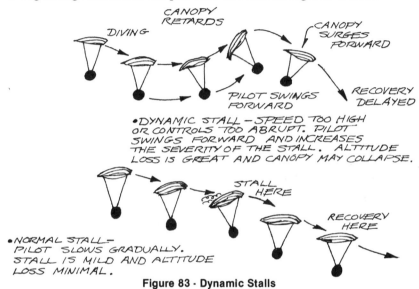

Figure 83 · Dynamic Stalls

Practice these stalls progressively until you know the behavior of your glider just prior to and after it stalls. Keep your stall gentle! Instant recognition and recovery from a stall can be the key to many happy returns in the sky. Of course, the best stall insurance is prevention. If you remember the commandment: *maintain thy airspeed* you will avoid our unwelcome guest, stalls.

TURN VARIATIONS

In Chapter V, we addressed simple correcting turns. Here we will explore full-blown intentional turns that allow you to write your name in the sky or auger down with impunity. We classify turns partially by the amount of brakes applied before the turn starts for this determines the response. Here we are assuming a two-riser system; in Chapter VIII we will learn to turn with a three-riser system.

OFF BRAKES (0% TURNS)

In this turn the glider is flying best glide speed or faster. To perform a turn in this configuration, simply pull down on one toggle. The canopy will respond by banking and arcing around the side that has the brake applied. Because of the forward speed, the path will be fairly open, but if this control is held the bank angle will increase until a steep spiral turn results.

After about 360° of turn, let up on the turn control and you may be able to stablize at a given bank angle. If you continue to hold the turn control, the bank will get quite steep and you will lose altitude rapidly for you are not coordinating the turn, but diving. These turns are called fast spirals and should be used carefully for the fast descent rates they cause (see figure 84). Of course, you should be familiar with this flight regime in case you need to come down fast near a thunderstorm.

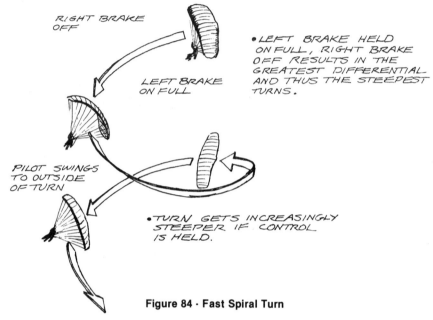

Figure 84 · Fast Spiral Turn

50% BRAKE TURNS
The 50% brake position results in turns that are much slower. To perform them, simply pull down on one toggle while maintaining the other in the 50% position. The glider turns very flat in this mode. To stop this turn, simply return the pulled brake to the 50% position.

75% to 100% BRAKE TURNS
With the brakes pulled to such a degree, the glider responds quickest of all. However, *the wing is very near the stall point* and great care must be exercised. It is best to "cross control" by relaxing one control line to about 25% as you pull the other. The turns in this case will be very efficient (minimum altitude lost for the amount of heading change desired).

Heres a *PRO-TIP*: To perform smooth and steady turns, maintain a constant control *tension*. This means you come off the control (toggle up) somewhat as the turn progresses and the speed builds up.

TURN PRACTICE
Every flight you take above a certain minimum (say 75 feet) should add to your turn practice. Besides varying the types of turns, you should prac-

104

tice turn exercises. Fly along a line (a road perhaps) and practice S-turns on either side of it as shown in figure 85a. Begin with 30° heading changes and progress to 180° turns eventually. Then try the same practice along a road oriented across the wind. You'll find you'll have to make different controls up and downwind, not because the glider reacts differently, but to maintain the ground track across the wind as shown in the figure.

CAUTION: Be extremely cautious when turning low to the ground for the pendulum effect may result in you swinging into the ground when you release the turn if you get too low.

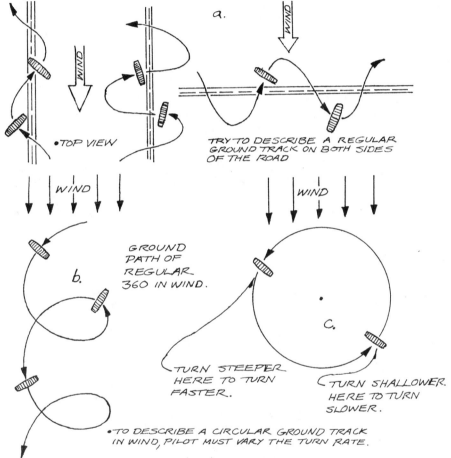

Figure 85 · Maneuvers in a Wind

The next thing to practice is 360° turns. Start out by obtaining plenty of clearance from the ground and your hill (say 500 ft-150m) in zero or light wind. Perform your first 360 then level out and think about what you felt. Then try another one and another, varying the direction. After you are comfortable with this practice, try linked 360s, adding them one at a time. Then try alternating their direction.

Notice how we approach this in a gradual manner. That's because 360s can be a problem. You can lose lots of altitude fast if you perform a fast spiral turn. Furthermore, you can become disoriented losing contact with your surroundings. This is called vertigo. Vertigo is a confusion that results when your inner ear balance equipment tells you something is happening with which your contentious eyes do not agree. In a steady turn centrifugal force evens out gravity to pull along your body's axis so your ear thinks you are at rest while your eyes say it ain't so. You build up your tolerance to vertigo by gradually building up the 360s you do.

The final thing to practice is 360s in a wind. Figure 85b shows you what happens if you perform a perfect coordinated 360 in wind. You drift and describe a spiral-like ground track. To turn a 360 over a given point in wind you must vary your turn rate or bank angle at different points as in 85c. The portion of the turn on the downwind side is fast and that on the upwind side is slow. This is great orientation and speed control practice.

LANDING PROCEDURES

Again we must complete the practice we began in Chapter V. Here we will learn how to perform a picture-perfect approach to landing.

There are basically two approved landing approach or set-up methods. The first is figure eights and the second is the aircraft approach.

FIGURE EIGHT LANDING APPROACH

The object of any landing approach is to put you in the right position to turn onto your final glide into your chosen spot. At the same time it should allow you to observe where you wish to land and make an easy position judgement.

In figure 86 we see a figure eight approach. Here the pilot turns back and forth to lose altitude. When he is the correct height above the field he turns to final and follows the landing procedures (speed, roundout and flare). There are three important things to note with this method. First, the pilot does not go beyond the downwind end of the field for fear of not penetrating back. Secondly, in light winds the pilot must make more than 180° turns to avoid creeping up the field and possibly running out of landing room as shown. Finally, the pilot must make the figure eights smaller as he gets lower to prevent getting caught to one side of the landing field without enough altitude to clear obstructions. Here's a summary:

Figure Eight Landing Rules
- Do not go beyond the downwind edge of the landing field.
- Turn figure eights with the amount of turn required to keep the ground track at the downwind edge of the field
- Make your figure eights shorter to remain within a 60° angle of your landing field.
- Use a fast final approach.

A variation on the figure eight approach is sometimes called the "tee" approach and is shown in figure 87. In this approach the pilot enters the pattern on the upwind side of the field and performs a series of figure eights that drifts him back to the far end of the field at which point he performs his final approach. This method is most useful in higher winds to overcome the potential problem of not being able to maintain a position

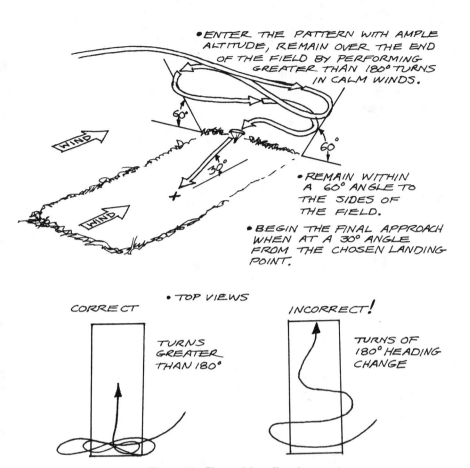

● ENTER THE PATTERN WITH AMPLE ALTITUDE, REMAIN OVER THE END OF THE FIELD BY PERFORMING GREATER THAN 180° TURNS IN CALM WINDS.

WIND

60°

60°

30°

● REMAIN WITHIN A 60° ANGLE TO THE SIDES OF THE FIELD.

● BEGIN THE FINAL APPROACH WHEN AT A 30° ANGLE FROM THE CHOSEN LANDING POINT.

● TOP VIEWS

CORRECT

TURNS GREATER THAN 180°

INCORRECT!

TURNS OF 180° HEADING CHANGE

Figure 86 · Figure 8 Landing Approach

over the end of the field. If you try this method in light or no wind, you will have to turn a little downwind on each 180 and this can be difficult. By all means practice this method over a wide open field the first few times. You should make each cross leg as long as possible so you aren't turning rapidly, but stay within reach of the field (see below).

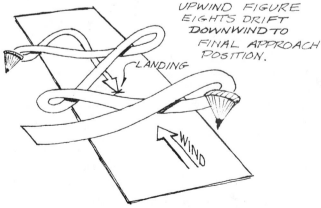

UPWIND FIGURE EIGHTS DRIFT DOWNWIND TO FINAL APPROACH POSITION.

LANDING

WIND

Figure 87 · Tee Landing Approach

AIRCRAFT LANDING APPROACH

There are three parts to this approach as shown in figure 88: a downwind, base and final leg. With this method you arrive at the upwind side of your landing field, then lose altitude by S-turns, figure eights or 360s (if you've practiced them religiously). At pattern height (about 100 feet—30 m), you enter the downwind leg, turn 90° to the base leg then another 90° to head into the wind on final to perform the landing procedure.

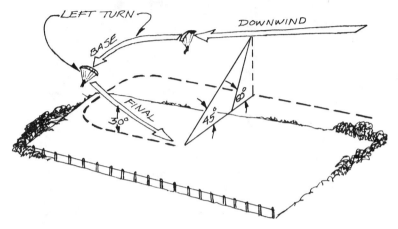

Figure 88 · Downwind, Base and Final Landing Approach

You can use left hand turns (the standard aircraft method) or right hand turns and should practice both approaches. You can vary your altitude along the way by altering your speed within limits (remember to maintain proper airspeed when close to the ground), the length of the legs or the amount of dive in your turns. To summarize:

> **Aircraft Approach Rules**
> • Lose altitude at the upwind side of your landing field.
> • Enter the downwind leg at a standard pattern height.
> • Turn on to base leg no later than the downwind edge of your field.
> • Vary your leg lengths or turns to control your altitude.
> • Use a fast final approach

With both of these approaches you are in a position to constantly view your landing spot. You should be totally familiar and practiced with both methods. Use the figure eight method in higher winds and the aircraft approach in lighter winds. This is because less heading change is required when turning figure eights in higher wind and the downwind leg takes place too quickly on the airplane approach in high winds.

Now here's a *PRO-TIP*: Don't try to judge your height above the ground in either approach—it is most difficult. Judge your angle to your chosen landing spot. Your eye has experience doing this. Try to remain about 45° to your spot on your downwind leg (aircraft approach) and 30° on your base or last figure eight leg as shown in the figures.

108

When you perfect these techniques you can move them to any landing field and perform a standard landing. That way you don't have to solve a new problem every time you fly outside your home port. You can also combine methods by inserting the figure eight pattern in place of the base (or crosswind) leg on the aircraft landing approach.

One other important rule we must make is necessary to prevent you from having penetration problems and missing your landing. That is:

> Maintain a 60° angle to your landing field when you are below 300 feet (90 m).

This rule is illustrated in figure 89 as well as 86, 87 and 88.

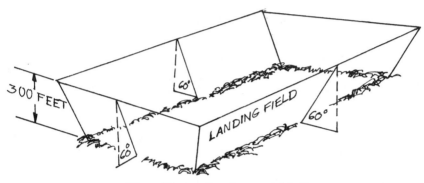

Figure 89 · Landing Approach Limits

Spot landing is an important skill not only to impress the natives, but also to make sure you can land where you must in tight situations. Use either of the above approach methods and practice, practice, practice. The secret to good spot landing technique is again using the angle method to

A good landing set-up leads to a good landing.

judge your position. You can use your brakes to vary your glide path on final approach, but be extremely cautious of flying slowly close to the ground and remember, if you approach too slowly you won't have any energy left to roundout or flare.

LANDING COMPLICATIONS ━━━━━━━━━━━━━━

Not all landings are by the book. Sometimes we misjudge or are inconvenienced by a wayward gust. We will look at what to do in this case. First, however here's how we minimize surprises: When you arrive at your site, check out the landing field for wind direction and consistency. Also look for any obstructions that may have appeared. We're not talking about a world record pumpkin, but how about cattle, plowed ruts or even a parked vehicle?

If you are flying a new site, check the landing field assiduously. Look for slopes and uneven terrain. Ruts or stumps hidden in long grass can be insidious. Look for possible rotor areas and powerlines. Finally, form an approach path in your mind. It helps to walk the ground path of this approach as you imagine the landing. Look for alternate set-ups if a wind switch occurs.

Windsocks and streamers should be placed strategically. Often pilots in the early stages of learning get confused about what the windsock are telling them. The simple rule is land from the tail to the mouth of the windsock.

At times it is nice to get a clear wind direction signal from pilots on the ground, especially in light winds that may not stir the socks. There is an unambiguous signal used by sport pilots as shown in figure 90. Here the signal person leans into the wind with his arms back to form an arrow and walks forward in the direction you should land. This signal was created because there was always embarassing confusion when some signalers pointed the direction the wind is coming from and some pointed the direction it is going to. You won't look graceful giving this signal, but you'll look less awkward than a pilot landing downwind by mistake.

• FACE THE WIND, LEAN FORWARD WITH ARMS BACK AND MOVE INTO THE WIND.

WIND

WIND

MOVE

• PILOT'S VIEW

Figure 90 · Wind Direction Signal

110

One of the major defenses a paraglider possesses is that it can be landed almost anywhere. Try to avoid powerlines and trees however as these items represent perhaps the greatest dangers. Practice your landing set ups and precision flares. This skills and judgement will stand you in good stead in those unexpected situations were everything you planned goes wrong.

DOWNWIND LANDINGS
It is always desirable to land into the wind, but sometimes you simply cannot avoid landing downwind if the wind is very light and changing 180°. The technique here is to come in with extra speed, round out carefully and flare hard to cause a dynamic stall to brake your body fully. You still may have to run a few steps because no matter what you do you can't reduce your groundspeed below that of the tailwind.

CROSSWIND LANDINGS
A crosswind landing is not too difficult if you are aware that your ground track is somewhat sideways. Your forward speed will be the same as in a calm wind landing if the crosswind is directly from the side, so a vigorous flare is in order. The only other thing to remember is to run sideways a few steps to offset your drift.

SLOPE LANDING
Landing on a downhill or side slope can be accomplished as long as you pay attention to timing. The slope may alter your perception somewhat as it drops away from you. Be cautious of the tendency to flare too soon on a downhill slope. We cover side slope landings in Chapter VIII.

An uphill slope is another matter. As shown in figure 91, your glide path and the slope combine to present a very steep approach angle. The only way to land successfully on an uphill slope is to flare hard with perfect timing to minimize your forward and downwind velocity. In truth, an uphill landing is an impact landing even if you can stop your forward speed for you have little energy retention. Remember, the slope can confuse your judgement and any headwind will be flowing downhill causing a greater sink rate then normal.

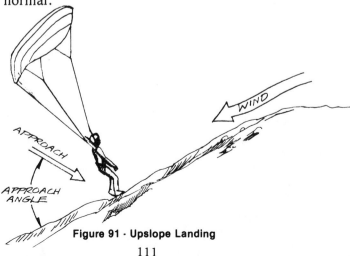

Figure 91 · Upslope Landing

If given a choice in hilly or undulating terrain, try to land across a slope, even in a crossing wind. The next best choice is to land downhill and the final choice is uphill. Each of these types of landings are more complicated than a normal flat ground landing, but the uphill landing is most difficult with the "hardest" results.

HIGH WIND LANDINGS

When you come down in high winds the problem is not so much how you touch down, but what you do after you touch down. When the canopy collapses behind you it becomes a drag chute that wants to introduce you to nature by dragging you through bushes, gulleys and cowpies. The remedy is to turn around the instant you touch down, run towards the canopy and pull the brake toggles down and back as shown in figure 92. An alternate method is to pull down hard on the rear risers. This will collapse the canopy at which point you should quickly grab all the connecting links and gather in the lines as you walk towards the canopy. When you reach the canopy, gather the leading and trailing edges in and throw it over your shoulder to lug it to a sheltered area.

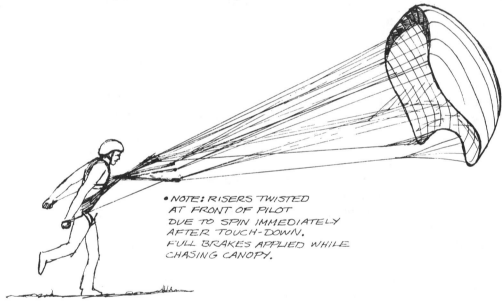

• NOTE: RISERS TWISTED AT FRONT OF PILOT DUE TO SPIN IMMEDIATELY AFTER TOUCH-DOWN. FULL BRAKES APPLIED WHILE CHASING CANOPY.

Figure 92 · Landing in High Winds

In any landing situation, misjudgement or sink can result in a hard touch down. For this situation we recommend the landing form shown in figure 93 a with the feet together for ankle protection and the knees bent to absorb shock. In very hard landings, this progresses to the parachutist's "landing roll" or PLR, which is designed to expend some of the vertical motion by translating it to horizontal motion. The roll sequence is shown in figure 93 a to g. Note the body is relaxed and the limbs are collected inward. The pilot is applying full brakes while he collapses to the side to land on his thigh and rear then roll over on his back to his other side. Practice this maneuver by dropping to the ground from a standing position then from a chair, then from a three foot stand.

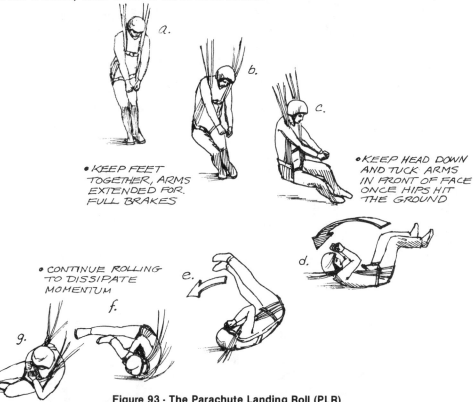

• KEEP FEET TOGETHER, ARMS EXTENDED FOR FULL BRAKES

• KEEP HEAD DOWN AND TUCK ARMS IN FRONT OF FACE ONCE HIPS HIT THE GROUND

• CONTINUE ROLLING TO DISSIPATE MOMENTUM

Figure 93 - The Parachute Landing Roll (PLR)

A pilot turns and collapses his canopy in high winds.

EMERGENCY PROCEDURES

Sometimes your day just doesn't go right even though you eat your Wheaties, shave with Gillette and use Right Guard deodorant. The unexpected can happen. But the consequences do not have to be too severe if we are prepared for them. Here we'll make that preparation by looking at several possible emergencies. Note we have already covered canopy collapse, brake entanglement and line entanglement in previous sections.

DEEP STALLS

Deep stalls are an infrequent occurence with our wings, but poor control input or intentional horsing around can create the situation. There is no mystery to a deep stall. It is simply a stabilized vertical descent. The problem arises from the fact that you are descending rapidly in a deep stall and probably some deformation of the canopy occurs. (Yes, you are in a parachute of sorts, but it's a pretty inefficient parachute in vertical descent mode. You need forward airspeed to produce lift with your airfoil shaped canopy. In a deep stall all you're getting is vertical drag.)

In figure 94 we see two forms of deep stall. The side views illustrate the differences and the airflow over the canopy both in the front and rear. It

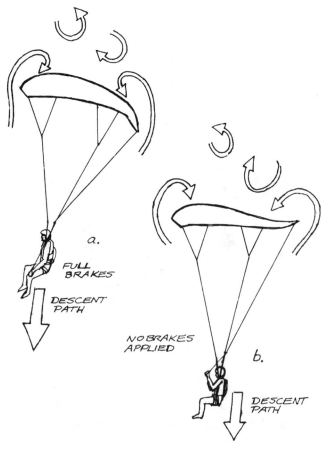

Figure 94 · Deep Stalls

can be seen that a deep stall occurs when the angle of attack is too high. This can happen with any combination of applying too much brakes and pulling on the rear risers, trimming the rear risers too much, sitting back in a steering seat (three-riser system) or encountering a sudden headwind gust.

In figure 94a we see a deep stall accompanied by full brakes applied. In this case releasing the brakes and pulling down on the front risers will lower the angle of attack and re-establish flying speed.

In figure 94b the brakes are not applied. In this situation the pilot must recover by applying full brakes to prevent the canopy from surging ahead (which can lead to a dynamic stall once the pilot swings forward). Hold full brakes to horseshoe the canopy which results in a quick drop and recovery of airspeed. Be sure to release the brakes gradually when the recovery occurs.

We must remind you that different gliders respond differently to various inputs. You should consult your owner's manual as to the specific recovery techniques in this and other emergencies. In general, the deep stall recovery procedures are:

1. Let off the brakes and rear risers or rear riser trim tabs. Move forward in a steering seat (three-riser system). Add a slight pull on the forward risers in a non-steering seat system.

2. Apply quick brakes (about half) to alter the flow over the wing and to keep the front of the canopy inflated and shift your body in front of the canopy. If the deep stall is not eliminated you can:

3. Apply full brakes to collapse the canopy and regain speed.

4. Apply one brake hard (75%) to enter a spiral turn.

The amount of altitude you lose will depend on the severity of your actions, which increase with the above steps. A full stall will always get you out of a deep stall, but you will lose the most altitude.

Note that a deep stall feels very much like encountering strong sink. The difference is in sink you still have forward flying speed and some turn control. Be sensitive to this difference by monitoring your airspeed and control response constantly. As in all emergencies of this nature, you must learn to detect the problem quickly so your remedial action results in little loss of altitude. For safety sake, avoid a deep stall by not using more than 50% brakes when closer to the terrain than 200 feet (60 m).

CANOPY OSCILLATIONS

In turbulence and gusty conditions, uneven forces on the canopy can cause it to oscillate in various manners. These oscillations are not terribly dangerous, but they should not be allowed to continue or they may worsen.

One type of oscillation occurs when the canopy rolls or swings from side to side. You may feel like you're being pulled from one side then the other in this case. To stop such an action as quickly as possible, raise your hands in two inch (5 cm) increments to release the brakes. Note the gradual change of controls. Quick control movements add to the instability of the canopy due to the interplay between canopy drag and your body's inertia.

The other type of oscillation that concerns us here is repetitive accordian action. In this case the sides of the canopy move in and out. You can stop this quickly by applying more brakes and turning into the wind. Although your wing does not detect the wind direction in a smooth wind, if turbulence exists it is rarely oriented the same in all directions. So adding brakes and heading upwind is the remedy here.

Remember, check your canopy frequently and the first thing to do when you feel a difference in the controls is look up to assess the situation. It should be clear that the above two problems require different solutions so you must first identify the problem.

TREE LANDINGS

In certain parts of the country, trees are the predominent ground cover. It is not unusual to find yourself over them if you fly in these areas. If you make an error in glide judgement, you may even find yourself in their leafy clutches.

Tree landings may seem humorous, but they are no joke as anyone perching in them can attest. If you find yourself bound to land in a tree, try to aim for the middle of the crown. The greatest danger is falling out of the tree once you hit. With any luck you will end up hanging in your harness safely above the ground. In this case you should wait for help to arrive because you run a much greater risk of falling once you unbuckle your harness.

The proper landing technique, is to cross your legs at the ankles to prevent broken legs and organs. Traditional parachutist technique is to cover your face with your hands, but with a paraglider, that precludes using the brakes to slow your descent. Perhaps the best compromise technique is to brake to as soft a landing as possible then quickly cover your face as you continue into the tree.

Once you have landed and arrived safely at the ground, you must think of your wing. Although it flies beautifully, it is most unbirdlike draped in a tree. The only way to get it out without inflicting more damage is to use a bow saw to cut branches progressively. If you try to pull the canopy out or cut the entire tree down you can probably say goodby to your beautiful wing or your wallet wad. Canopy repairs are costly. Use a lot of patience and care.

POWER LINE LANDINGS

Power lines are dangerous because they can knock you out of the sky but can also zap you in the process. You should suspect them anywhere you see a road, building or cut in the ground cover. Often their poles are hidden in trees, so it pays dividends to be familiar with all the fields near where you fly.

If you are going to contact a power line, keep your hands and your feet in to avoid touching the line. If you get hung up in them, don't move, but call for help. Any miscalculation can cause a life-threatening arc. Let the power company come and turn the power off before you try to extricate yourself.

WATER LANDINGS

Wet landings can be hazardous to your health if you are fully clothed and wrapped in a harness and canopy. Here are the procedures to handle such a mishap. First, undo your chest buckle before you hit. This should be done at least 150 ft (46 m) above the water. Remember, that's only 20 to 30 seconds before you hit. Next head into the wind so the canopy falls behind you. Just as you hit take a deep breath and release the leg straps or climb out of them (depending on the harness). Once you are free of the harness, swim upwind away from the canopy to avoid entanglement. Don't worry about your glider—it will float like a big jellyfish and you can retrieve it later. Here we review water landing precautions:

Water Landing
- Fly with float gear and a hook knife when near water
- Stay away from surf for it will greatly complicate your escape from the canopy
- Unbuckle your chest strap well above the water
- Land heading into the wind
- Take a deep breath and remove the rest of the harness
- Swim away (upwind) from the glider

The most important thing is not to panic. You will float even with your clothes on so don't be too hasty and lose your ability to work effectively.

CONTROL LINE BREAKAGE

This emergency can be well prepared for ahead of time by simply practicing controlling the glider by pulling on the rear risers. You can control direction by pulling on one side and speed by pulling both. In the case of this emergency, make your landing approach with a long straight final and flare by pulling down hard on the rear risers with the same timing as normally. Be cautious of pulling to hard on the rear risers during flight as you can create a severe stall in this manner. Flying with the risers was covered earlier in this chapter.

PARACHUTE PROCEDURES

Many pilots who learn to soar and regularly fly in more challenging conditions choose to fly with a parachute. If you do acquire one, it isn't much good unless you know how to use it. Assuming it is a hand deployed model, here are the steps for maximum percentages:

Parachute Deployment
1. Look at the deployment handle.
2. Grasp the handle.
3. Look for a clear area.
4. Pull down and out to free the parachute from the container.
5. Throw the parachute into the clear area in the direction of any spin present.
6. Pull hard on the parachute bridle.
7. Retrieve the parachute and rethrow it if necessary.

Some of these steps seem elementary, but they all have a purpose mainly to insure you grab the right thing and throw to the right place. If you are spinning you can wrap up the parachute so you should try to throw it into the spin.

You should maintain your parachute by caring for it exactly as you do your paraglider. Don't sit on it, keep it dry and store it cool. Also you should learn to repack your chute and do this at least every six months to maximize the opening potential.

A WORD ABOUT SAFETY

You've come a long way since you first heard about paragliding and acquired the desire to fly. You now have the magic to float into space on a whim. But as you survey all that's behind you there's still that vast body of aviation knowledge ahead of you. You get a taste of it every time you fly and a thermal hits or a pilot makes a comment about lift bands and soaring. The challenge is still there and it keeps on getting better.

However, we must caution you on one point. Overconfidence is a common deadly fault that often creeps into a pilot's demeanor once he or she has mastered the basics. Don't ever take the attitude that you know all there is about a facet of flying and don't ever refuse to listen to someone critiquing your flying even if you deem them of lesser skill than you. We can all use constant feedback concerning our skills and judgement whether we are beginners or experts.

Finally, we will leave you with a sad item that has proven true throughout all forms of aviation:

> The most dangerous pilot is the one flying for family, friends or cameras.

We can turn this around by realizing the part that ego and pride play in our sport then make a mature decision to fly within our limits. That is not to say that our limits can't be expanded with practice and experience. That's exactly what we want to achieve.

SUMMARY

You've worked long and hard to get to this stage of your flying career. You can't say it hasn't been fun. While you may be goal oriented, you must admit that the passage was a great time.

And now you have arrived at the first step to becoming an expert pilot. If you have absorbed all the information and completed all the practice to here, you should be capable of passing the APA Novice rating tasks and test. We direct your attention to this material in the Appendices of this book and wish you luck.

Of course, you will continue your learning in the remaining chapters of this book. Until you progress further, we offer the APA recommended limitations for Novice pilots. You should exceed these limitations only after demonstrating mastery of the required Class I tasks and after acquiring a comprehensive understanding of potential problems and dangerous situations which may arise at a given site.

Novice Operating Limitations

- Always wear a helmet
- Never fly alone
- Try one new thing at a time
- Fly with visual contact of your landing zone
- Fly in winds 12 mph (19 km/h) or less with a gust factor less than 5 mph (8 km/h).
- Fly only from slopes between 4:1 and 1:1
- Launch with wind 30° or less from straight in.
- Perform turns of 45° or more at an altitude of 200 ft. (60 m) or greater.

Enjoy your place in the sky.

An afternoon glide in Washington state.

*Evening air can provide
a magic flight.*

*Landing after a soaring
flight in the Alps.*

CHAPTER VII

The Rules of the Air

As you take your place in the sky you will begin to feel as free as a bird. And in truth you are, for you have very little but the laws of nature to restrict you. However, even the birds must be concerned about avoiding other air traffic. If they weren't we would see some mightly confused flocks.

It is for our own safety and benefit that we understand and obey certain simple traffic rules. These rules not only keep us from hitting each other by providing a standard procedure for everyone to follow (so there's no shuffling back and forth like two people meeting head-on in a hallway) but are also obeyed by aircraft of all sorts which is comforting indeed.

Other rules we will cover are those relating to certain areas of airspace through which we are prohibited from flying. These rules are mainly for our protection because there is much air traffic in these areas. To an airplane zipping through the sky, we are sitting ducks. It is very unrewarding to back up through the engine of a 747 at 300 mph.

First we'll begin with a few social considerations.

SITE PROTOCOL

Most of the sites we fly are provided for us by the good graces of the landowners, government, and site managers. Sites are fragile entities. They also require a lot of work and sometimes money to maintain.

It is up to every one of us to help preserve sites or we will be spending most of our time either driving long distances to the few ones we retain or dreaming about the sport we no longer can practice due to lost areas. Our personal behavior at sites is important. We are individual representatives of our sport and must realize that our behavior will determine how the public perceives paragliding in general. As much as we do not want to be ruled by public opinion, the facts of life dictate that the public does partially control our right to fly through the passing of laws and allowing us the use of sites.

It should go without saying that we must be sure to pick up all our trash at a site, but also clean up that of spectators and party people that regularly frequent isolated overlooks. If we don't, land owners may view us as an attractive nuisance. Other less obvious precautions are parking vehicles in a manner that doesn't block traffic and refraining from driving across sensitive fields or landing in crops.

Many potential flying sites are previously secured hang gliding sites. Some of these are quite restricted in terms of the skill level of pilots who may fly the site as well as landing fields and access. It is important for all paraglider pilots to understand the necessity of contacting the local hang gliding community to find out site availability and rules. All forms of sport aviation must band together if we are going to maintain our freedom. With the proper approach, paraglider and hang glider pilots can form an alliance that enhances both sports in terms of public relations, site control and social interaction. Imagine your reputation if you ignore such logic and permanently lose a site for both hang gliding and paragliding!

RIGHT OF WAY RULES

Here we present the standard rules that allow us to operate with order around other flying objects. These rules should be understood, memorized and obeyed at all times. They are based on common sense and have prevented many a potential midair collision.

THE RULES

1. *Aircraft approaching head-on should steer to the right of oncoming traffic* (figure 95a). This rule is not hard to remember since it is the same rule you follow with a car in the U.S.

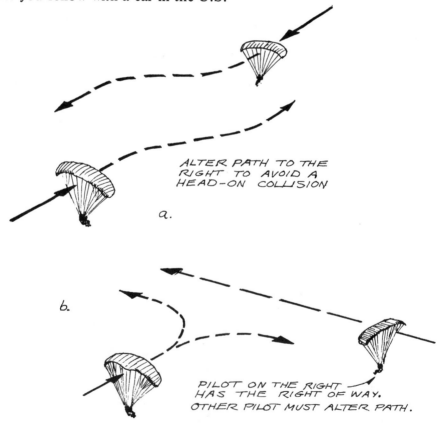

ALTER PATH TO THE RIGHT TO AVOID A HEAD-ON COLLISION

a.

b.

PILOT ON THE RIGHT HAS THE RIGHT OF WAY. OTHER PILOT MUST ALTER PATH.

Figure 95 · Approach Right of Ways

122

2. *A glider approaching on the right has the right of way* (figure 95 b). *The pilot on the left must give way.* However, don't use your right of way to force a pilot to alter course uneccesarily. Again this rule is the same for automobiles.

3. *When ridge soaring, the glider closest to the ridge has the right of way* (figure 96). The pilot next to the ridge cannot turn towards the ridge. This rule supercedes rule 1.

4. *When ridge soaring, the low glider has the right of way* (figure 96).

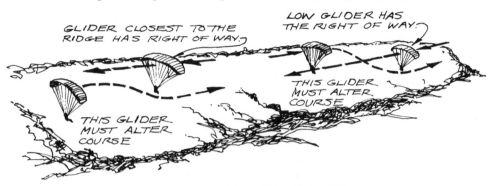

Figure 96 · Close and Low Glider Right of Ways

5. *When ridge soaring, always turn away from the hill when reversing directions* (figure 97). This rule keeps you from hitting the hill but also lets everyone know which way the other pilot will turn.

6. *When ridge soaring, a glider overtaking another glider flying the same direction should pass between the ridge and the glider being overtaken* (figure 97). This rule is necessary because of the previous one. A glider reversing direction will turn away from the hill and may hit you if you are passing on the outside.

Figure 97 · Overtaking on a Ridge

7. *When thermaling, the low glider has the right of way* (figure 98). This rule is simply because the low pilot cannot see the higher pilot while the upper pilot can see. Note that this is the opposite rule to that of sailplanes since they can look up best.

8. *When thermaling, the first pilot to enter a thermal establishes the turning direction for all other pilots entering that thermal* (figure 98).

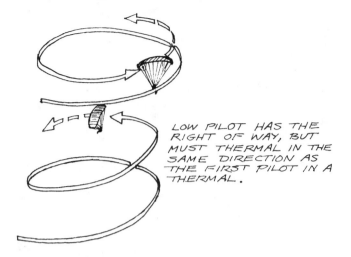

LOW PILOT HAS THE RIGHT OF WAY, BUT MUST THERMAL IN THE SAME DIRECTION AS THE FIRST PILOT IN A THERMAL.

Figure 98 · Thermaling Right of Ways

Whether you come in below or above the other pilot, turn the same way so you don't conflict if you get to the same level and other pilots will know which way to turn when they enter the thermal.

9. *Don't fly directly over another glider with less than 50 feet (15 m) clearance.* This is to prevent a midair in case the lower glider encounters lift before you do.

10. *Paragliders must yield right of way to all other aircraft except powered ultralights.* This is discussed in Section 103.13 below.

11. *Paragliders must comply with the FAA Federal Aviation Regulation Part 103* (FAR Part 103).

The last two rules are Federal rules which we review below. The last flying rule for use in glider traffic is simply: clear your turns.

FAR PART 103

In 1982, the FAA instituted special rules governing ultralights, both powered and unpowered, which includes paragliders. Up until that time matters were for the most part unregulated. Below are the main rules that relate to Paragliding. All pilots should understand them well, for violation is punishable with a $1,000 fine for each infraction.

Applicability

Section 103.1 of FAR Part 103 defines an ultralight vehicle. It turns out that paragliders are unpowered ultralights according to the federal government. There are several criteria we must meet as listed below:

a) Single occupancy. Paragliders can carry one person only, except under an exemption. To fly tandem legally you must meet certain qualifications and achieve a special tandem rating. Write the APA office for the forms and procedures.

b) Recreation purposes only. You cannot receive compensation for your flying in any way. However, situations that do allow you to make money are instruction, rental of equipment, sporting events, authoring books (fortunately for us) and receiving discounts on equipment. Aerial advertising is specifically prohibited. You *can* fly with a company logo and may even get a free glider in the deal, but you cannot enter into an agreement that specifies the location, number or pattern of flights. You cannot fly for hire in airshows or public exhibitions.

c) Airworthiness Certificate. If you want to fly for hire or otherwise avoid some of the rules in Part 103, you may obtain an airworthiness certificate from the FAA. This will take some doing, but it has been accomplished on several occasions. Write the FAA for Advisory Circular 20-27C.

d) Weight limits. A paraglider must weigh less than 155 pounds. That means we can use a canopy big enough to carry a horse!

Inspection Requirements

Section 103.3 says that you must allow an FAA official to inspect your glider for compliance with Part 103. Furthermore, you must provide any documentation necessary to prove this compliance. In the field, if an FAA official approaches you with specific requests of this nature, we suggest you exercise courtesy, for they have the power of arrest and the usual human reactions to questions of their authority. Don't expect this to happen, however, unless you violate some airspace rule.

Waivers and Certificates

Section 103.5 says you can only conduct operations that deviate from Part 103 by obtaining a written waiver. To obtain such a waiver, contact your GADO (General Area District Office). Remember, you are dealing with masters of red tape, so you need patience and luck. However, many of these officials are curious about paragliding and may go out of their way to help you.

Section 103.7 says that our gliders are not required to meet any federal government airworthiness standards nor are they required to be registered or bear markings. Furthermore, pilots are not required to be licensed or have any experience, knowledge, age, or medical qualifications.

Since the above section was written, however, the FAA has pushed for the voluntary compliance with a three-part program: vehicle airworthiness, registration and pilot registration (presented in Advisory Circular 103-1). The APA has been charged with administering this program for paragliding.

Since Part 103 was developed, the FAA has added new airspace restrictions for airplanes that they have indicated apply to paragliders also. These are ARSAs (Area Radar Service Areas) that appear around medium size airports. You should get an aviation sectional chart (available at airports) for your area and learn where you can and cannot fly. Your life may depend on it.

Hazardous Operations

Section 103.9 prohibits operations such as flying or dropping of objects so as to create a hazard to persons or property. The interpretation of hazard is vague—intentionally so—so that you can be fined if your actions are perceived as a threat to the public. Certainly, diving at spectators on launch, crashing into someone's car or landing in a mature corn field could lead to a fine under this ruling.

Daylight Operations

Section 103.11 states that you can only fly from sunrise to sunset. That's legally defined sunrise and sunset which may be found in your local newspaper or an almanac. All those moonlight flights or our favorite pastime of watching the sunset from the air are hereby prohibited. The only exception to this rule is a 30-minute extension before sunrise and after sunset if you display a blinking anticollision light which is visible for three miles and you remain in uncontrolled airspace (below 1,200 feet above the terrain in most places).

Right-of-Way Rules

Section 103.13 determines who has the right-of-way in ultralight operations. Simply put, paragliders must yield right-of-way to all aircraft except powered ultralights. The law treats paragliders, hang gliders, ultralight balloons and other unpowered ultralight craft as equal. There is no right of way defined under the law between these vehicles. Even one of these vehicles under distress does not have right of way in the U.S.

Congested Area Operations

Section 103.15 prohibits flying over a congested area of a city, town or settlement or an open air assembly of persons. This is another catch-all ruling. In the past, a congested area has been defined as one house. Thus, if you make it a habit to fly over a nude sunbather in the privacy of their back yard, they can complain and have you fined. Skirt habitations on your way to a landing field and avoid landing in city parks that require you to fly over buildings.

Operations in Controlled Airspace

Sections 103.17 and 103.19 prohibit the operation of paragliders in cer-

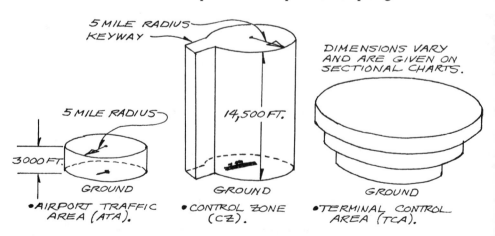

Figure 99 · Restricted Airspace

126

tain areas of controlled airspace (see figure 99). These are Airport Traffic Areas (a cylinder 3,000 feet high with a five mile radius around airports with an operating control tower), Control Zone (an area around high volume airports that extends up to 14,500 feet above sea level), Terminal Control Area (around large airports), Positive Control Area (above 18,000 feet), Prohibited Areas and Restricted Areas (the latter two are usually around military operations and national monuments). You can get a waiver to operate in any of these areas but you'll need some luck in many cases.

Visual Reference with the
Surface and Cloud Clearance

Section 103.21 states that you must maintain visual reference with the surface at all times. Simply put, that means you cannot fly in clouds or even above a stratus layer or extensive fog bank.

Section 103.23 defines the cloud clearance requirements. There is some logic to this: pilot flying airplanes on instruments have their eyes glued to the panel when they zip through the clouds. They exit horizontally, so it may take a good distance before they focus on their environment and start looking for other air traffic. You wouldn't have a chance if an airplane popped out of a cloud and aimed for you from a hundred yards away. The other consideration is that cloud bottoms tend to be fairly level while the tops tend to billow.

With these three criteria you can remember the cloud clearance values as: 2,000 feet horizontal, 500 feet below and 1,000 feet above (see figure 100). This holds true except above 10,000 feet and outside controlled airspace (below 1,200 feet in most areas). Outside controlled airspace you

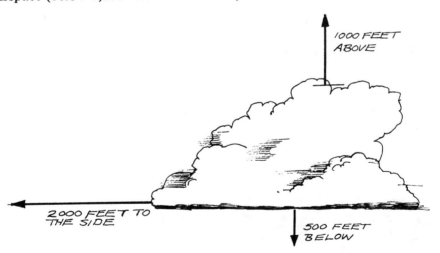

Figure 100 · Cloud Clearance Requirements

must remain clear of clouds and visibility must be at least one mile. In all other areas visibility must be at least three miles.

Again we note that cloud flying is illegal (and dangerous). Also, getting to cloudbase is likewise an illegal act.

127

Section 103.20 requires all pilots to be aware of notams (notices to airmen) by calling Flight Service (see the phone book under Federal Government, FAA). These notams may restrict airspace in the vicinity of important personages.

From the preceding you can see there are several ways to end up having to spend your lunch money on insidious fines. The most likely rules you'll run afoul of are hazardous operations, flying over congested areas and cloud flying.

SUMMARY

We have outlined the social and legal rules that govern our flying. Laws of any sort can be considered to be restricting (especially that of gravity), but even the most devout anarchist obeys common sense rules like not walking into doors. Those who don't use common sense experience evolution in action by eliminating themselves from the gene pool.

Most of the laws pertaining to our flying are based on common sense. We can live with them both figuratively and literally. A little wisdom and care will keep us out of the path of the "heavy iron" and in our own blissful volume of airspace.

CHAPTER VIII

Finding the Lift
Intermediate Skills

By the time you have achieved your Class I rating, you are well aware that there is more to this sport than meets the eye of the casual spectator. You have perhaps seen pilots soaring aloft and making flights with precision control in more tricky conditions. Maybe you have admired their skills and composure in the air. By chance you long to become such a superior pilot.

We're going to start you along the way to this goal in this chapter. But first we must admonish that accepting greater challenges invites greater risks so the wise pilot must be mature enough to know his or her limits and take the time to learn new skills on a gradual basis. Furthermore, we wish to leave you with another aviation maxim that will serve you well to remember:

> "The superior pilot uses his superior judgement to avoid using his superior skills."

ADVANCED EQUIPMENT

Part of the skills acquired by a more advanced pilot should be the familiarity of flying with the various type of equipment available. Some of this equipment will be designed for more advanced pilots because it requires more advanced skills to operate safely. Here we will take a look at equipment differences and how they affect our flying techniques.

As mentioned in Chapter II, one of the characteristics of advanced canopies is the higher aspect ratios used in the design. This normally results in nine, eleven or more cell canopies. Because of greater efficiency related to higher aspect ratios, the gliders can be flown at a higher wing loading. Thus, in general, high performance canopies are of smaller area yet they get the same sink rate and a superior glide compared to beginner and intermediate designs.

Often these advanced designs take off faster because they are smaller or they are trimmed to fly at a lower angle of attack than other gliders. This may result in the canopy getting ahead of the pilot on takeoff. On some advanced designs, normal takeoff procedure requires you to apply brakes—as much as 50% to effect a lift off. This is not too difficult to learn, but requires some practice to perfect the timing. It is highly recommended that learning to take off with such a glider take place with a smooth wind to assist you.

Other problems with advanced designs is that they may collapse easier both straight ahead and in a steep turn. Furthermore, they may require more pilot input to recover from a collapse.

Advanced canopies can further exhibit quick control response which may take a little time for the pilot to learn. They are more sensitive to your control inputs. Again, the gradual approach is expedient here with turns progressing from half-brake turns to off-brake turns well away from the terrain in gentle conditions. Note that the flare timing is often more critical in advanced designs so your first landings should be in a smooth wind of at least 5 mph (8 km/h).

Other differences we may mention are various crossports between cells, airfoil alterations and Mylar plastic canopy sections as well as trailing and leading edge tape to minimize stretch. All these items are performance features and do not affect the actual control too much, but one item that does is any arrangement that allows the pilot to alter the angle of attack directly by adjusting riser length.

An advanced glider demonstrating closed cells at the wing tips.

THE STEERING SEAT

In Chapter II we briefly mentioned advanced harness types that allow the pilot to adjust his or her weight position and thereby alter the amount of weight on the front or near risers. This effectively alters the trim angle of attack of the glider. By shifting forward the pilot puts more weight on the front risers to lower the canopy's nose and thus speed up. The opposite effect occurs with the weight shifted backwards. We call this harness a steering seat.

Flying with a steering seat allows a pilot to directly change angle of attack without using brakes and thus leads to better performance. Contemporary steering seats employ three or four-riser systems as shown in figure 101. This schematic shows how the front riser is attached to the seat and forms a pivot while the rear risers are allowed to float up and down according to the pilot position which changes angle of attack. (The four-riser system is similar with the extra riser routing to the ''B'' lines.)

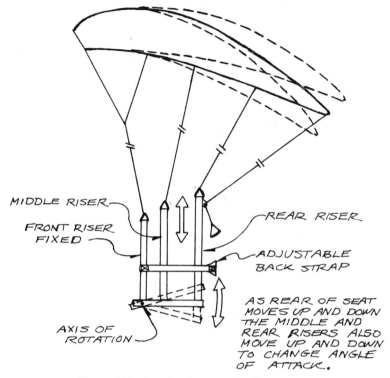

MIDDLE RISER

FRONT RISER
FIXED

REAR RISER

ADJUSTABLE
BACK STRAP

AS REAR OF SEAT
MOVES UP AND DOWN
THE MIDDLE AND
REAR RISERS ALSO
MOVE UP AND DOWN
TO CHANGE ANGLE
OF ATTACK.

AXIS OF
ROTATION

Figure 101 · Steering Seat Mechanism

To adjust a steering seat, tighten the leg straps so the front risers are placed at the crease between your buttock and hamstring muscles when in sitting position as in figure 102. Try sitting on a chair with the harness on, or have a couple strong friends lift you with the risers so you can feel the adjustments and find the neutral position as shown in the figure.

Your sitting position should be erect, so adjust the lumbar (back) strap accordingly. The shoulder straps should be just snug and the chest strap just barely snug to avoid pulling the risers inward and changing the angle of incidence.

The flying positions in a steering seat are shown in figure 103, a to c. The neutral position is shown in 103a. Here the canopy is in its normal trim at best glide and you should feel quite at home. Note, you may have to consciously hold your legs up to maintain this position on your initial trials with a steering harness.

The sitting back position (103b) is achieved by lifting the knees straight up. Do not lean back too far or you effectively pull down on the front risers as you pull the lumbar support. This may speed the glider up rather than slow it as is normal for this position. With the knees up, the angle of attack increases, more camber is in the canopy and minimum sink rate is achieved.

131

In figure 103c we depict the fast position with the legs extended. The proper position is again with the torso erect (do not lean forward). This position results in a flatter airfoil in the canopy, a lower angle of attack and thus more speed, more maneuverability and a higher stall speed.

In turbulence, the front of the canopy can fold under at this low angle of attack. You can recover or prevent this situation by applying brakes (up to 50% for prevention, more for cure). Be cautious of flying in the full forward position with full brakes, for lifting the legs will result in a dynamic stall.

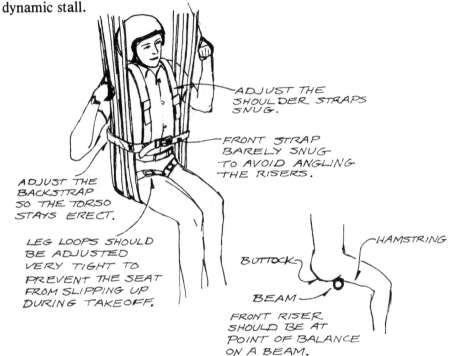

ADJUST THE SHOULDER STRAPS SNUG.

FRONT STRAP BARELY SNUG TO AVOID ANGLING THE RISERS.

ADJUST THE BACKSTRAP SO THE TORSO STAYS ERECT.

LEG LOOPS SHOULD BE ADJUSTED VERY TIGHT TO PREVENT THE SEAT FROM SLIPPING UP DURING TAKEOFF.

HAMSTRING

BUTTOCK

BEAM

FRONT RISER SHOULD BE AT POINT OF BALANCE ON A BEAM.

Figure 102 · Adjusting a Steering Seat

LAUNCHING A STEERING SEAT

The takeoff with a steering seat is a bit different than that of a conventional (two-riser) harness for the arms are held lower due to the low attachment point on the risers. Figure 104 shows the takeoff sequence

In 104a the pilot has stepped back two paces from the point of line tautness to provide momentum as the canopy begins to inflate. Note the initial arm positions with elbows bent and upper arms in to the sides. The arms are pulled forward and up as inflation progresses.

When the canopy sails over the pilot's head the resistance decreases. When the canopy is straight up the pilot must come off the risers and apply a little brake (a few inches of pull) to prevent the canopy from moving forward and deflating. With the pilot in running position, the front risers are pulled down so the brakes must be applied to prevent a dive (see 104b).

As with all systems, you must look up to preform your preflight check while you steady the glider above you. Continue running until you are in the air. *Don't jump and don't sit down.* The takeoff position is the for-

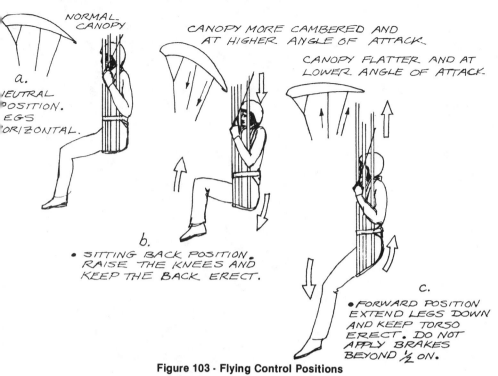

NORMAL CANOPY

CANOPY MORE CAMBERED AND AT HIGHER ANGLE OF ATTACK.

CANOPY FLATTER AND AT LOWER ANGLE OF ATTACK.

a.
NEUTRAL POSITION. LEGS HORIZONTAL.

b.
• SITTING BACK POSITION. RAISE THE KNEES AND KEEP THE BACK ERECT.

c.
• FORWARD POSITION EXTEND LEGS DOWN AND KEEP TORSO ERECT. DO NOT APPLY BRAKES BEYOND ½ ON.

Figure 103 - Flying Control Positions

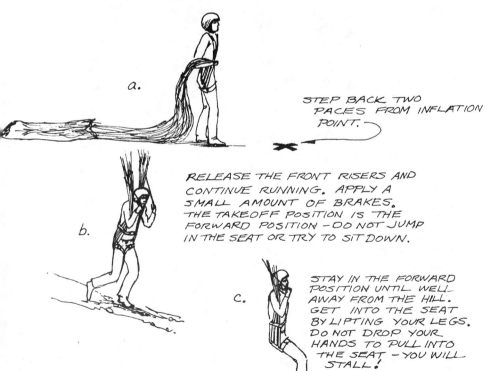

a.

STEP BACK TWO PACES FROM INFLATION POINT.

b.
RELEASE THE FRONT RISERS AND CONTINUE RUNNING. APPLY A SMALL AMOUNT OF BRAKES. THE TAKEOFF POSITION IS THE FORWARD POSITION - DO NOT JUMP IN THE SEAT OR TRY TO SIT DOWN.

c.
STAY IN THE FORWARD POSITION UNTIL WELL AWAY FROM THE HILL. GET INTO THE SEAT BY LIFTING YOUR LEGS. DO NOT DROP YOUR HANDS TO PULL INTO THE SEAT - YOU WILL STALL!

Figure 104 - Launching with a Steering Seat

ward position and light brakes must be applied (unlike a two-riser system) in order to take off. Stay in the forward position until you are well clear from the terrain (see 104c). Use only the brakes for steering until you are in the neutral position.

To achieve the neutral position, simply lift your knees. Caution: *Do not drop your hands to help you slide into the seat and do not hold onto the risers to pull yourself up.* You will stall in the first case and dive in the second. Simply lift your knees. If you have trouble getting into the seat with this operation then most likely the leg straps are too loose. Keep them as tight as possible.

Launching with a steering seat. Note lower arm position.

TURNING WITH A STEERING SEAT

Because the risers are directly attached to the seat, you can angle the canopy and effect a turn by angling your body. This produces a more efficient turn for you are not simply stopping one side with the brakes like a bulldozer, but actually carving a turn. Note: an experienced pilot can also steer with a regular board seat, for shifting the weight effectively shifts the alignment of the upper harness. However, this practice is not nearly as effective as when an actual steering seat is employed.

Here are the steps to produce a left hand turn as shown in figure 105. First speed up by dropping your legs. Next, lean with your hips while keeping the head and torso vertical to bank the glider. Then lift your legs to slow the glider to coordinate the turn. Your outside leg is lifted more than the inside leg. Note the body angulation and arm positions. If you wish to tighten the turn you can apply more angulation or add a little brake on the inside side. Experiment with variations of bank angle and brake application to see how your glider reacts to all situations.

To end the turn you simply level your hips and sit upright. You can use a little brakes on the outside to help you dampen any oscillations.

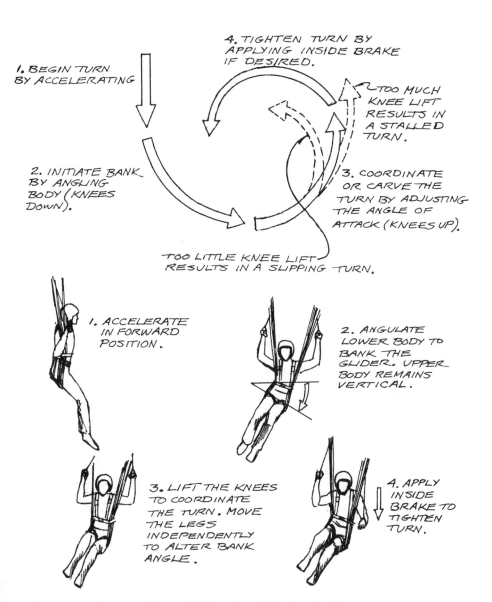

Figure 105 · Turning with a Steering Seat

LANDING WITH A STEERING SEAT

Close to the ground you are not trying to achieve the utmost in efficiency, so make all steering turns with the brakes. About 30 feet (10m) above the ground, assume the forward position to gain speed for flaring and offsetting the wind gradient. Release the brake pressure except for steering corrections (note if turbulence exists, maintain about 25% brakes and bring the legs up to neutral position to slow down and minimize the chance of a deflation).

About 10 feet (3 m) from the ground lift your knees to neutral position in a gradual manner to effect a roundout. Be sure to lift the knees together to avoid all maneuvering with the seat. When you are about 3 feet (1m) from the ground extend your legs to absorb shock and simultaneously apply full brakes to slow your descent. Extending the legs lowers the angle of attack and speeds up the glider, so don't do it too soon and be sure to apply full brakes so you don't leave a bad impression on the ground. Figure 106 shows the landing sequence.

An alternate method of landing with a steering seat consists of lifting the knees to slow the wing just before touchdown, but this can lead to a stall as you apply full brakes and you are not in a good position to absorb the landing shock. Use this method with caution or stick to the former landing technique.

Needless to say, becoming familiar with a system such as this should take place only in gentle conditions with lots of time between takeoff and landing. All new equipment should be first tried at your friendly training hill.

Figure 106 · Landing Sequence

WIND AWARENESS

As we fly longer we become tempted at times to fly in higher winds. Of course, we are aware that there is an upper limit to the winds we can handle. This limit is imposed by two factors: the penetration of our gliders and the increased turbulence associated with higher winds.

The maximum safe flying speed of most gliders is from 17 to 25 mph (27 to 40 km/h), depending on the wing loading and design. Obviously if we fly in wind greater than this speed we will be in reverse gear. We had better carry along an anchor in this case. In all seriousness, winds near our maximum flying speed can pose grave dangers, even if they are smooth due to the existence of venturis (see below) and rotors near a hill. A wise limit for pilots of advanced skill is to fly in smooth winds no higher than 80% of their maximum safe speed. In variable conditions or with lesser skill, the limits are lower. We summarize:

> **Maximum Wind Limits**
> •In smooth winds with advanced skills, limit winds to 80% of your maximum safe penetration speed.
> •In gusty conditions, reduce this limit to 50% with a maximum gust factor of 5 mph (8 km/h).
> •An Intermediate pilot should set a limit of 15 mph in smooth conditions regardless of penetration capabilities to maintain a safety margin.

As we have learned in Chapter IV, turbulence is associated with wind moving over and around obstructions. Generally, the more wind and the larger the obstructions, the greater the turbulence. We expect more turbulence from an upwind hill than a house, and less still from a car, for example. Consequently, we usually find a seaside site to exhibit less turbulence in a higher wind than an inland site, both because the sea air is more stable and there are no obstructions upwind of a site looking out to sea unless a blue whale breaches. In fact, the only place it may be reasonable to fly in winds at the upper levels of your glider's capabilities may be a site facing a large body of water (or possibly a wide open plain on a cool day).

We mentioned stable conditions and a cool day above because the sun's heating produces thermals or unstable conditions which greatly increases the turbulence. We will review thermals below when we discuss soaring, but the reader should reread the section entitled *TURBULENCE—WASHBOARD AIR* in Chapter IV that deals with both thermal and shear turbulence as well as wake and mechanical turbulence.

One other factor that affects mechanical turbulence besides wind velocity and obstruction shape is the air's density. When the air is more dense it has more force and energy in a given velocity gust. Thus we can say that winter turbulence is more virulent than that of summer due to the greater density of cooler air. However, winter conditions are normally much more stable than summer conditions so there's a trade-off involved. Sometimes the winds of winter can be glassy smooth. Furthermore, the denser air of winter results in less actual wind velocity required to soar a given site because of the greater force exerted by the "heavy" air.

When the air is more stable with little or no vertical movement we call this "laminar air." Although laminar air can be very smooth, it exhibits two tendencies that we must understand. First, laminar air is most likely to produce the strongest venturi effect (see the next section). Secondly, laminar air and stable conditions in general produce the most dramatic wind gradient effects due to the lack of mixing at ground level. We must be particularly sure to carry good speed on landing approach in windy, stable conditions.

WIND AND THE TERRAIN

Before we move on to more challenges, let's get a clearer picture of the air's curious behavior in different situations. The first two effects will mention are rotors and venturis. Rotors as we have already illustrated in

Chapter IV occur downwind from certain sharp obstructions in a steady wind. Of course, if a rotor doesn't remain in one place, it breaks off and becomes a moving eddy or swirl which is just as bad from our piloting point of view. Rotors should be expected behind any large or long obstruction. They can be behind our takeoff or hill as illustrated in figure 107.

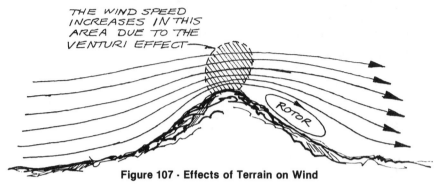

Figure 107 · Effects of Terrain on Wind

Another item illustrated in the figure is the venturi effect. This effect is the increase in wind speed near the top of a hill due to the "squeezing" of the air as it tries to move up over the hill. This is similar to water in a stream accelerating as it is forced around a boulder that constricts the stream. Venturi effect is real and common and should be well understood by all pilots. Flying in upper level wind invites the risk of blowing backwards if the pilot is careless enough to drift into the venturi area.

In general, we should expect a wind gradient near takeoff just as we encounter one in the landing area. Figure 108 shows how this gradient can

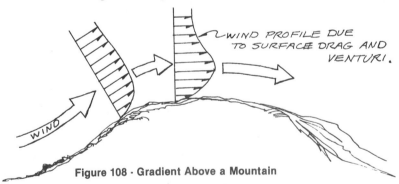

Figure 108 · Gradient Above a Mountain

combine with the venturi into exhibiting less winds at takeoff than we are likely to encounter further up in the air. The following rule should help remind you of this:

Maximum Wind Velocity
Wind above a ridge is usually a maximum just above the peak (highest part) of the ridge and will reach this maximum from 50 feet (15 m) to several thousand feet, depending on the upper level winds. The wind will be lower just in front of the ridge and reduces as altitude is lost.

Remember, if you get caught in a high wind the emergency procedure is to pull down (carefully) on the front risers to speed up. Also, if winds are too strong at takeoff you can usually move down the hill, but be cautious of getting carried back up to the higher wind level in soaring conditions. Watch your groundspeed carefully and speed up if you feel yourself drifting back to a trouble area.

An extreme form of wind gradient is known as a wind shadow. This is usually caused by an abrupt drop-off in the terrain or ground cover (trees) and is most prevalent when an entire area is sheltered from the wind such as a field surrounded by trees. This is shown in profile in figure 109. This extreme form of gradient can cause a severe stall if you descend through it with too little airspeed. In wind shadow conditions as with any wind gradient, acquire and maintain good airspeed before you hit the strong gradient area.

Figure 109 · Wind Shadow

On another note, we have previously discussed the daily upslope and downslope breezes. At night you can be surprised by a downhill breeze at takeoff despite a day of good uphill breezes. All this usually creates is a bit of disappointment, but when you are on landing approach the change in wind direction can be dangerous if you are not aware of the possibility. As a general rule of thumb:

Evening Winds
•Expect reverse winds in your landing area at the end of a day of strong solar heating with little upper wind
•The higher the mountains, the nearer you are to the base of the mountain and the closer you are to a ravine or canyon, the more frequent and stronger this effect will be.

Late in the evening a closed or narrow valley can exhibit other related phenomenon. The trickling of cool air down the mountain sides can form a pool of air lifting the warmer air it replaces. This warm air is very bouyant and blows up the face of the mountain in a form of great lift called "wonder winds." This is shown in figure 110.

At other times, the air may cascade down both sides of the valley to meet in the middle to rise and form widespread lift known as "magic air." With this knowledge we would do well to understand that flying along the sides of a canyon (on the side facing the prevailing wind) would be the ex-

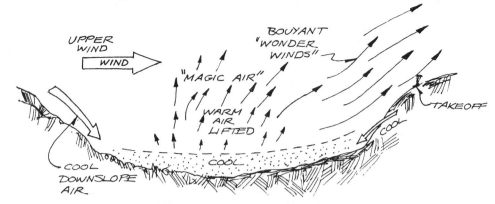

Figure 110 · Wonder Winds and Magic Air

pedient path during the day while flying over the middle of the canyon in the evening with catabatic (downhill) flow present along the sides is the wiser choice if we are trying to maintain altitude or glide far. This is illustrated in figure 111 for both cases.

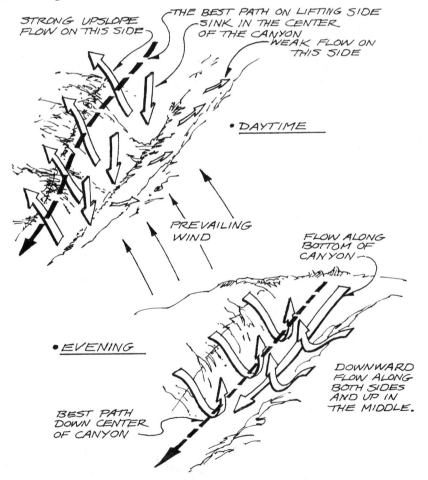

Figure 111 · Upslope and Downslope Breezes

140

In some valleys or some clear sky evenings with fast cooling, the cool pool of air that forms from the air sliding off the mountains will act like a well of inertia and form a shear layer at the interface where it meets the moving warm air above as shown in figure 112.

Figure 112 · Evening Shear Turbulence

In some situations with a sloped valley floor the cool air that pools in the valley in the evening slides downward along the valley to form a brisk breeze that produces strong turbulence where it rubs against the overlying warm air and strong winds that are much faster at the surface than above this layer. This is a common occurance in the high, close valleys of the Alps.

The alert and observant pilot will be aware of all of these effects as well as others to either take advantage of the gift of lift they offer or to avoid them for safety reasons. The reader is directed to our companion book *Flying Conditions* that can be ordered through the publisher's address at the front of this book. *Flying Conditions* covers large and small scale weather effects for sport aviators.

ADVANCED TAKEOFFS

In this section we look at more difficult takeoff situations with an eye towards determining the possibilities, describing techniques and defining our limits. Here are a few different types of takeoff.

CROSSWIND TAKEOFFS

In Chapter VI we learned how to handle crosswind takeoffs in mild winds with up to 30° of cross. Here we'll extend this to stronger winds and up to 45° of crosswind. Actually, in stronger winds your canopy will inflate and be maintainable above your head with control input for stability. If the wind is cross you can inflate your canopy while facing directly into the wind then turn your body to face downhill and begin running while allowing the canopy to adjust to your flying direction. An alternate method is to run across the hill. However, with a shallow slope, running across the hill makes it more shallow. A steeper slope may also cause problems since you'll be running with one leg virtually shorter than the other. If the terrain permits, perhaps the best crosswind technique in windy conditions is to split the difference between the wind direction and the fall line of the hill (straight down the slope) and run in that direction so as to avoid over-controlling and being blown along the hill away from the wind. Figure 113 illustrates this concept.

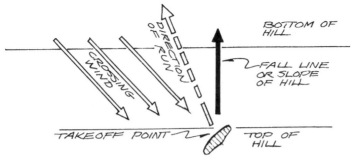

Figure 113 · Crosswind Technique in Stronger Winds

HIGH ALTITUDE AND TAILWIND TAKEOFFS

We group these two special conditions together for the technique to mastering them is essentially the same. At high altitudes the air is less dense and therefore more airspeed is required to inflate the canopy and gain lift for flying. This translates to more running speed and distance. A rule of atmospheric physics (sky science) states:

> **Airspeed At Altitude**
> The air density decreases about 3% per thousand feet. This results in an increase in all speeds of 1.5% per thousand feet, including takeoff speed. As an example, a sea level takeoff speed of 15 mph (24 km/h) would increase to 16.8 mph (27 km/h) at 8000 ft (2438 m) which is an 8 x 1.5% or 12% increase.

In a similar manner, a downwind takeoff requires additional running speed (and room) to make up for the loss of airspeed the glider feels due to the tailwind. Obviously there is a limit to how much tailwind can be tolerated. This is less than a few miles an hour (a mere trickle) tailwind for most pilots. You can check your ability to handle a tailwind by trying to inflate your canopy on flat ground with a slight rearward wind component. Whatever wind you can handle on the flat should be reasonable on a slope where you can run easier.

However, the red light signal should be flashing in your brain. On a slope you can't stop too easily if you have a canopy malfunction or your canopy doesn't inflate. The extra speed required in a tailwind launch could lead to an embarassing and painful tumble down the hill as you roll up into your canopy like a snapped window shade.

CAUTION: Do not attempt a downwind or tailwind takeoff in wind greater than 3 miles an hour (5 km/h) or on a slope steeper than you care to fall down.

In general, the ideal situation for taking off is with the wind directly up the hill. If this is not the case, we must be very careful to stay within the bounds of our known limits. These limits are best established at a training hill in a controlled environment.

CLIFF LAUNCHING

Cliff launches introduce an element of danger due to one thing: the cliff. If your paraglider isn't inflated by the time you reach the edge of the cliff then you're in for a cataclysmic encounter with the third planet. A cliff launch in calm conditions requires enough running room before the cliff to inflate, flight check and abort takeoff if necessary before reaching the cliff. Any wind moving up the cliff face may aid your takeoff or may demand all your control and concentration as you hit a wall of air at the cliff edge. In figure 114 we see a cliff launch in light winds depicted. This assumes 5 mph (8 km/h) and less winds.

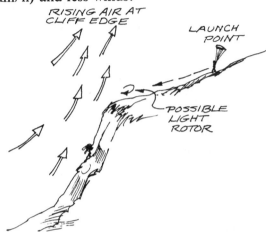

Figure 114 · Light Wind Cliff Launch

In figure 115 we depict a windy cliff situation. Here the problem is the presence of rotors and gustiness behind the lip of the cliff. It is often not possible to inflate a canopy and penetrate out into the smoother air with any margin of safety. Some pilots have launched by sitting on the edge of a cliff, inflating and leaping, but this is an extremely dangerous undertaking for even if it is successful one day doesn't mean it will be successful on another due to the changeable and unpredictable nature of cliff edge turbulence. Rotors can actually push your canopy forward or a heartless gust

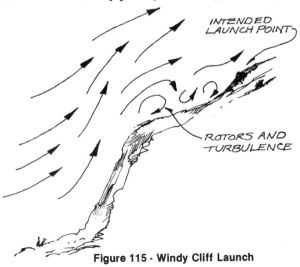

Figure 115 · Windy Cliff Launch

can collapse your canopy just as you leap into space.

CAUTION: We discourage even expert pilots from launching from a shear cliff in winds over 5 mph (8 km/h).

Again we repeat: cliff launches are dangerous. With the added element of strong winds they can be downright deadly due to the difficulty of maintaining and assuring a stable canopy in the launch phase.

CRITICAL TURNS—FAST SPIRALS

One other facet of flight we are going to take a step further for the advancing pilot is turn control. We mentioned fast spin turns in Chapter VI. Here we will review the technique and indicate its uses. First, you will recall that a fast spin turn is built up after several revolutions or 360s with one brake pulled up to 70% and the other brake completely off. This provides the greatest differential in brakes from side to side and therefore the potential for the greatest turn forces.

With an optimum single brake deployment about 50%, the canopy can be held in a stable, very fast spin descent. The control action must be smooth and a bit of gradual release may be necessary to keep the same angle of bank and spiral rate. Note that the G forces will build up and the canopy may distort somewhat in this maneuver so some control adjustment may have to be made as the spiral stabilizes. This activity was previously pictured in figure 84.

The most useful purpose of such a fast spiral is to lose altitude quickly when so desired. When one is in the clutches of cloud suck (powerful lift) one finds such techniques and the practice thereof most gratifying. Demonstrating such turns is a requirement for a Intermediate rating so learning them is a must for aspiring air aces. Start them gradually (with slight control) then increase both the number of revolutions you attempt and the control input. Remember, the greater the control and the longer you hold it, the faster and steeper will be the resulting turn. Be sure to release the control gently.

Note that many modern, high-performance gliders will not maintain a fast spiral without collapsing the inside wing. If this is the case, the best way to lose altitude quickly is with staged collapses of the canopy. This technique is covered after the next section. In any case, you should consult your owner's manual or ask your dealer to find out the optimum operating procedures for your particular wing.

STALL TURNS

Stall turns are another matter entirely. They are produced by pulling down hard on one control, especially if both brakes are already deployed from half to full. A stalled turn results in the canopy dropping back relative to the pilot, artificially increasing the angle of attack as shown in figure 116. The pilot describes a small arc during this maneuver while the canopy follows a wider circle around him.

A stalled turn loses altitude very rapidly and should be practiced with plenty of clearance and caution. Remember, a stalled wing is not a good thing in turbulence, so try this new turn in smooth air. Learn to perform stalled turns if you will, by the sensible gradual method. Start with slightly stalled turns (smaller and less vigorous control deflection) then progress to deeper stalls (one wing only!).

To recover from such a turn, smoothly release your controls to off-brakes (both sides). Your glider should roll out of the turn and resume flying speed by itself.

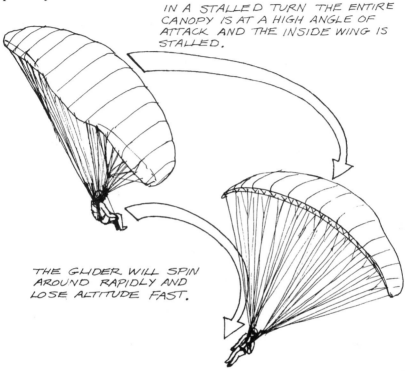

IN A STALLED TURN THE ENTIRE CANOPY IS AT A HIGH ANGLE OF ATTACK AND THE INSIDE WING IS STALLED.

THE GLIDER WILL SPIN AROUND RAPIDLY AND LOSE ALTITUDE FAST.

Figure 116 · Stalled Turns

ADVANCED STALLS AND ALTITUDE LOSS

In Chapter VI we covered a "deep stall" which is a flight regime the pilot enters usually inadvertantly and which affords little control. Here we investigate two other forms of stalls that a pilot can produce that are just as radical.

The first is a dynamic stall as shown previously in figure 83, Chapter VI. This stall results when the angle of attack is rapidly increased or brakes are rapidly applied when the glider is flying with some airspeed above stall speed. The canopy is retarded and the pilot swings forward to increase the angle of attack even more. This sort of severe stall is not recommended as canopy collapse may occur and much altitude can be lost during recovery.

The second severe form of stall is a full horseshoe stall (see figure 117). In this case the brakes are held full on until the canopy folds up behind us. When performing such a maneuver, two extremely important things must be considered: Both brakes must be pulled identically and much altitude will be rapidly lost. The canopy will collapse if this configuration is held, so allow yourself at least 1000 feet (300 m) of ground clearance for your

145

initial trials. If you do not pull both brakes uniformaly the collapsed canopy may become entangled and requires even more recovery altitude. Releasing the brakes effects a recovery in properly designed gliders.

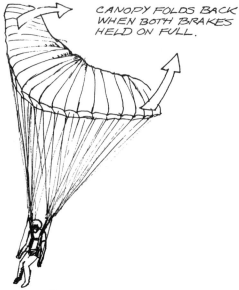

CANOPY FOLDS BACK WHEN BOTH BRAKES HELD ON FULL.

Figure 117 · Horseshoe Stall

We go into detail concerning the full horseshoe stall because many pilots use this method to lose altitude rapidly in an emergency situation, most, notably, cloud suck. Indeed, in some high-performance gliders this is the only way to lose altitude in an emergency since tight spirals are not advised (see above).

In general, canopy collapse should be a repetitive process of collapse, fall, recover in successive stages to prevent excessive speeds and high forces from building up. High-performance canopies especially are difficult to hold in the collapsed state without folding taking place. With careful controlled collapse and opening you can achieve a high average descent rate and maintain the integrity of your canopy.

We caution you to practice this maneuver with plenty of altitude and be wary of causing a canopy collapse in strong turbulence for it may wrap up the canopy before it can reinflate.

COMPLICATED LANDINGS ─────────────────

Once you learn precise control of your wing you may wish to experience other skills. One of these is landing on the side of a hill. This is a an Advanced requirement and is useful for emergency landings and uneven terrain.

The technique for a side hill landing is quite straightforward. Approach the intended landing spot directly across the slope as shown in figure 118. If you are in wind you will have to crab so that your ground track is across the slope. If there is no wind your canopy should be pointing directly across the slope.

146

Figure 118 · Side Slope Landing

Your goal is to blend into the terrain by flying along the hill while running more and braking less than normal on a flat slope landing. You must control your flight path so that you stay on the slope. Be sure to land in the direction facing any quartering wind and apply a little more brake on the uphill riser to prevent you from edging away from the hill and treading air.

Remember, don't use too much brakes in a side hill landing or you will be too high in stall configuration. When it comes time to collapse the canopy, do so by pulling the uphill brake so it falls into the hill and tends to keep you planted. Watch your run on the uneven terrain so you don't twist an ankle.

A type of landing that is a bit more involved is a landing on top of a hill during soaring (see below). We will assume you are soaring a gentle hill with plenty of clearance above the top of the hill and a wide open area on top in which to land. If this is not the case then these landings shouldn't be attempted. If it is the case, then look at figure 119. Here we see the classic

Figure 119 · Top Landing Procedure

method for landing on the top of a soarable hill. The pilot uses his altitude to drift back over the lip of the hill then turns into the wind to land.

The best way to perform this feat safely is to not turn downwind to drift back, but start from the side of your intended landing point and reduce your crab angle until you drift back to the desired point. That way you will only have to produce a 90° turn to head into the wind and thus avoid a dangerous downwind landing if you hit unexpected sink.

Other complications include having too much altitude once you get back there and the possibility of encountering turbulence. If you do have too much height, simply perform figure eight turns to come down, being cautious not to creep towards the front. In fact, your early trials at landing on top should be with extra height so you have plenty of time to judge your position and clear any expected rotor or turbulence.

The main problem with landing on top of a hill is the turbulence associated with winds behind a sharp change in terrain. As shown in the figure, this turbulence (and a rotor) will extend some distance back from a sharp lip. Wind streamers should be placed in your intended landing area so you can tell if turbulence is present before you attempt such a landing. A smooth, rounded hill is the best candidate for top landing as are light, bouyant evening winds. If you have any doubts about the safety of conditions, don't attempt this advanced feat.

Since your canopy is a good ways above the terrain it is possible that it will be out of the rotor or turbulence present at the front of a gently changing slope. In this case you may land right at the slope edge. However, explore this possibility cautiously by inflating and maintaining your canopy in the general intended landing area.

Landing close to the front of a slope is tricky since you must maintain some speed to penetrate the wind, yet you want to degrade your performance. A careful playing with the brakes is necessary. In any case, you must do a high wind landing (turn around, collapse the canopy and chase it) since conditions by definition are soarable.

An ideal hill for a side slope or top landing.

LEARNING TO SOAR

The term soaring, properly applied, refers to sustaining flight by means of ascending air currents above the normal glide path of an aircraft. When we speak of soaring we simply mean staying up in lift.

This soaring business is some fun. On a good day you have time to relax and really take in the view. Your first soaring flight will change your perspective on things. We suspect that soaring is closer to the dream of flying that most of us share than any other mode of flight.

Unfortunately, soaring is not without its demands or hazards. In order to soar you must have a vertical wind velocity equal to or greater than your sink rate. If, for example, your minimum sink rate is 400 feet per minute, a vertical wind of 400 feet per minute will sustain you. This is only 4.5 mph (7.2 km/h), but the wind is rarely vertical. Normally it blows at an angle up the slope of a hill or mountain, so its vertical component must be equal to or greater than this magical 4.5 mph and the overall wind will be stronger.

Figure 120 illustrates the situation on a 30° slope. For a vertical component of 4.5 mph to exist along this slope, the actual wind must be twice that or 9 mph. And this is just barely sustainable flight. For the purpose of gaining altitude or staying aloft with ease, more wind is required. As we know, more wind means more chance of turbulence.

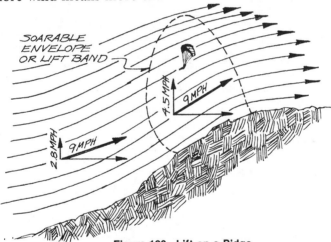

Figure 120 · Lift on a Ridge

The type of soaring we have described here is known as ridge soaring because we are riding upward currents deflected by a ridge or mountain. Because of the higher winds required for ridge soaring, it should only be attempted by expert pilots with the understanding that it takes place near the limits of safety.

The other common source of lift is thermals. We will describe them in more detail below, but here we must mention that thermals present their own problem—namely turbulence. So soaring in a paraglider is not without risk, but you can minimize this risk by carefully assessing the conditions and learning soaring skills gradually. Certainly, some days exhibit ideal conditions for soaring with smooth bouyant winds, big benign thermals or both.

RIDGE SOARING

Ridge soaring is the most basic form of extended flight. It is the first type of soaring you may experience because the possibility exists any time the wind is blowing above 5 mph (8 km/h). It is also the easiest to understand. In figure 120 we illustrated how lift is produced by a slope. In this figure we extend our understanding to see that the lift near a mountain is not everywhere the same. In fact, there is a relatively small area above and in front of the slope where the vertical component is great enough to keep us up. This area is called the lift band or soarable envelope.

In order to remain in this lift band we must fly parallel to the ridge as shown in figure 121. To do this we must crab to the left and right. If we fly straight out from the ridge we will soon be out of the lift band. If we direct our glider parallel to the ridge we will be blown over the top. The crab angle is directed more perpendicular to the ridge as the wind velocity increases. The amount of lift available depends on the following:

Ridge Lift Factors

1. The angle of the slope—the steeper the better.
2. The height of the slope—the higher the better.
3. The length of the face—the longer the better. A ridge is much better than a hill since the air can go around the hill instead of over it.
4. The strength of the wind—the stronger the wind the better, up to about 20 mph (32 km/h).
5. The angle the wind hits the hill—a perpendicular wind is best. The lift drops quickly as the wind begins to cross.

You can begin your ridge soaring practice on a day that isn't really soarable by turning after takeoff to fly parallel to the ridge. What you are trying to learn is to stabilize and turn soon after takeoff and to follow the ridge. Try to perform a 180° turn and follow back along the ridge. At all

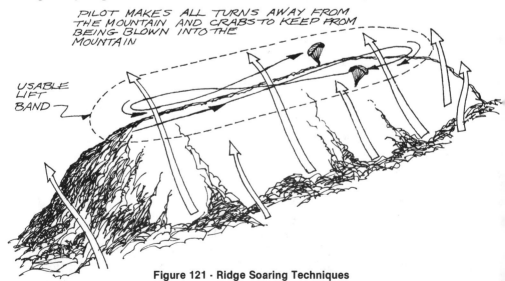

Figure 121 · Ridge Soaring Techniques

times be aware of your position with respect to the ridge (you will be sinking and will have to move out) and your landing field (allow plenty of arrival altitude).

Once you have accomplished the above, repeat the same process in more wind. Remember, always build your skills gradually to insure safety.

Your first attempts at soaring should proceed with a turn to parallel the ridge once you are well clear of the ground. Make a pass a couple of wingspans away from the terrain and fly at an airspeed offering you good control. After several trials, gradually learn to slow down and fly a little closer to the ridge. Note that even expert pilots cannot fly at minimum sink speed when they are close to the ridge top if turbulence occurs.

If you begin to rise, maintain your position in the lift band and continue to parallel the ridge. Once you are well above the top you may be able to move closer to the ridge to exploit the best lift. Make your turns smooth and shallow to minimize altitude loss. If you turn out of the lift band, continue turning a little more until your glider is aiming parallel to the ridge and you drift back into the hill. Once you're repositioned readjust your heading to stop the drift and follow a path directly along the ridge.

If the wind is somewhat across the ridge your progress in one direction will be faster than that coming back because you will have a tailwind component one way and a headwind component the other way. We call this "fast beat" and "slow beat" flying.

You do not have to do anything particularly different going one way or the other in a crossing wind, since your crab angle to the hill is the same (because you are offsetting the same wind component perpendicular to the ridge) but you do have to recognize the headwind component for what it is and resist the tendency to fly too fast to try and make progress. Furthermore you must recognize the tailwind pass and avoid getting too far away from a safe landing field with no penetration when you turn back into the wind.

In general, when the wind is cross at takeoff you should make your initial turn into the wind to avoid overbanking. Once things have settled down and you have a little terrain clearance you can then turn toward the downwind cross direction if so desired.

Your initial actual soaring attempt should take place in smooth winds from 8 to 12 mph (13 to 19 km/h). Perform a well-controlled takeoff and a careful turn in the lift band. Watch your airspeed and position and you should have no problems.

Of course, you won't be perfect in your early attempts, so here are some potential problems to consider:

1. Turning too late on take-off. Most beginners wait too long to turn and thus fly out of the lift. One note of caution: always turn in the direction of the wind on take-off if it is crossing. The reason for this is there is a wind gradient close to the slope which can roll you into the hill.

2. Turning too often. If the lift is very light it will take time to rise to maximum height. A turn always loses more altitude than minimum sink flight. In marginal lift conditions, make your passes long with few turns.

3. Flying too far away from the ridge. When you first learn to soar you may be fearful of getting too close and thus not fly in the best lift. Flying

too close to the ridge is of course dangerous. The best lift is over the steepest part of the slope.

4. Flying too fast. Your best sink rate is at a speed just above a stall. In very light lift without turbulence you must fly this speed constantly. Do not stall however. At best you will lose plenty of altitude recovering. At worse you will be blown back into the hill since you have no control in a stalled condition. This, of course, can be quite dangerous.

5. Gaps and breaks in the ridge. These are outlets for the wind so there is a lot of air rushing through them. Be ready for this and angle away from the ridge to cross them. Often you will notice no difference when crossing a gap, but be prepared for stronger winds.

6. Getting too far back above a ridge. When the air is forced up over a ridge there is an area of faster moving wind just above the ridge due to a venturi effect when the wind is horizontal. Avoid this area by remaining in front of the crest of the ridge. (In upslope thermal winds this problem doesn't occur as much, but beginning soaring pilots do not have the experience to judge the difference in such conditions.)

7. Getting too far from your landing area. A new soaring pilot can get caught up in the ecstasy of staying aloft for the first time and drift too far away from the landing field. Remember that on some days lift can quickly shut off—especially in the evening—so keep a safe distance from a good landing field.

Once you learn to ridge soar you can perfect your skills by trying to imagine where the best lift is located and locating yourself accordingly. You can venture a ways away from your normal takeoff-to-landing flight path (but always rerain in safe reach of a landing field) and begin to explore the sky.

THERMAL SOARING

Using thermal lift is a bit more difficult than using ridge lift. To see why, we must investigate the nature of a thermal. Look at a pan of boiling water. See the bubbles forming? They adhere to the bottom while they grow, then break off to rise briskly to the top. The exact same process occurs in nature. The sun heats up certain surfaces quicker than others and produces bubbles of hot air which grow, then break off and rise. A pilot can learn to detect this rising air and circle in it while he climbs higher. Watch a hawk's lazy circular flight. If you see him gradually going up then he has "hooked a thermal".

The surface areas that produce thermals best are parking lots, plowed fields, dried grass areas or bare rocks. These areas are heated much more readily than vegetation which tends to dissipate the heat. The size of the thermal is determined in part by the size of the area producing it. Higher winds will tend to break the thermal away before it grows large.

An ideal thermal appears as in the drawing in figure 122. Note that the greatest velocity is in the center or core of the thermal. There is an area of downdraft around the thermal and possible turbulence. When a wind is present the thermal may not be so nicely formed, but leans with the wind and becomes eroded. Some thermals are bubbles limited in vertical extent and some are columns that are thousands of feet high. This feature

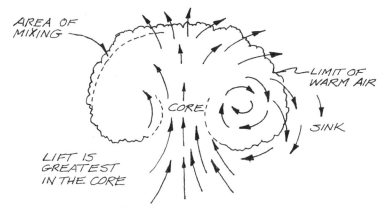

Figure 122 · The Ideal Thermal

depends on the amount of warm air supply on the surface and the intensity of the solar heating.

A thermal will rise until the air cools to the point that any moisture it contains is condensed and a cloud forms. This is the familiar cauliflower or cotton puff cloud. Thermals can exist without producing clouds if the air is dry. These are called "blue thermals".

You have probably already flown into thermals and experienced their bumps and lift (see figure 123). The technique is to circle or turn figure eights in the middle of the thermal. Since we cannot see a thermal this isn't easy. One solution is to use instruments. These are altimeters and variometers as described in Chapter II. When you are in strong thermals you can feel the initial upward acceleration, but if you continue steadily upward the senses can no longer detect the upward movement. This is where a variometer becomes a handy tool. In light, "scratchy" thermals a "vario" is indispensible for mapping and exploiting lift.

If you don't have a variometer, try using all your senses to find the lift. Often when passing into a thermal the air will feel warmer or even carry

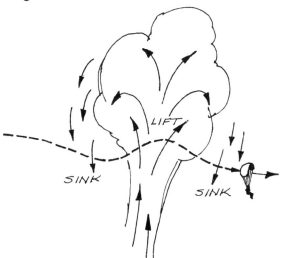

Figure 123 · Lift and Sink Around A Thermal

153

scents from below with it. The thermal drifts with the wind, so learn to watch your ground track and vary it accordingly. The first indicator of a thermal will be a bump of varying severity. If you are off to one side of the thermal you may be turned away. Quickly turn towards the lifted wing and find the center. Once in a thermal, find the area of maximum lift by tightening your circle or figure eight as lift gets weaker and opening your turn as lift increases (see figure 124). Practice exploring thermals every time you encounter one well clear of the terrain and soon you will be able to center in the lift and continue to climb in steady circles.

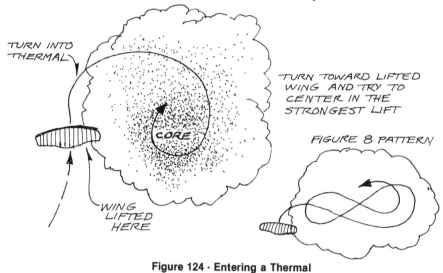

TURN INTO THERMAL

TURN TOWARD LIFTED WING AND TRY TO CENTER IN THE STRONGEST LIFT

FIGURE 8 PATTERN

CORE

WING LIFTED HERE

Figure 124 · Entering a Thermal

Once you enter the thermal, you circle or turn figure eights to stay within the lift and ride as high as you can go. This may be from several hundred to tens of thousands of feet. On any given day the thermals can be of many different sizes and strengths. A good pilot will be flying back and forth like a shark looking for a meal.

Experienced pilots often combine thermal soaring with ridge soaring. This is because they need the ridge lift to stay aloft until they find a thermal. A ridge or hill is a thermal collector. The reason for this is a thermal will drift with the wind. A light thermal may be rising only a few feet per minute while a strong thermal can produce several thousand feet per minute lift. The top of the thermal rises about half the actual upward velocity of the center (see figure 122). Thus, the thermal will often have a great sideways drift and be blown into the ridge (see figure 125). Once it hits the ridge it is deflected upward. In this manner, a large number of thermals from various distances away from the ridge will be concentrated along the slope. On a good thermal day you can often ridge soar even though the actual wind is low.

For now, you should allow yourself plenty of clearance when turning in thermals (review the section on 360's) and maintain a 1 to 1 glide (45° angle) to the front of your hill when drifting back in thermals. Keep good maneuvering speed in the air, especially when close to the terrain. We will discuss clouds and thunderstorms below as well as avoiding other air traffic. Here is a list of hazards involved with thermal flying:

Thermal Hazards
- Turning 360's close to the terrain.
- Drifting over the back of the mountain.
- Possibility of strong turbulence.
- Flying into the clouds.
- Thunderstorm encounters.
- Other air traffic.

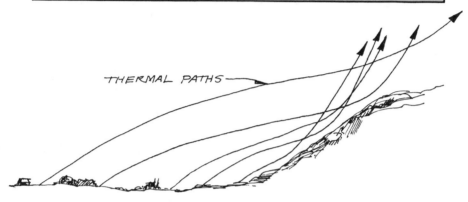

Figure 125 · A Ridge Collecting Thermals

WAVE LIFT

There are other forms of lift that soaring pilots may exploit. These are wave lift and convergence lift. Briefly, waves are produced just like ripples in water downstream from a sunken log. The waves rebound from a mountain and continue moving up and down for a considerable distance downwind of the mountain that forms them as shown in figure 126. Evidence of waves can be seen in the flat "lenticular" wave clouds that occasionally form high in the sky.

Flying in waves with a paraglider is a tricky proposition at best for they are often associated with stronger winds. Waves can be as smooth as fresh cream or rife with gut-wrenching turbulence. Most likely the only place you will encounter a wave will be on an evening ridge soaring flight. If you are in gentle,

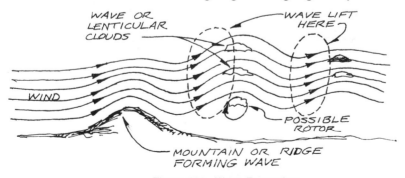

Figure 126 · Wave Formation

155

light and steady lift that extends much higher than normal ridge lift, you can bet you're being "waved aloft". The only thing you need to worry about is rising into stronger winds that drift you backward. If this happens, descend into lower winds and stay in front of your mountain.

CONVERGENCE LIFT ───────────────────────

To converge means to come together and that's exactly what the air does to cause this lift. Two air masses can come together at the top of a high mountain producing upslope breezes on both sides. This is often evidenced by a cap cloud that doesn't drift with the wind but continuously sits above the mountain top (see figure 127). We have already mentioned the lift produced when air slides down both sides of a valley and meets in the middle. This too is convergence. When the flow along two valleys meet, the air produces convergence lift. If a general wind is blowing toward a large water body, the seabreeze formed during the day will meet this general wind and converge.

Since the air is always moving from a variety of causes, we should expect convergence to take place often. Unfortunately, most of this convergence lift is too weak for us to exploit. We can rarely go looking for it since it is less predictable than ridge or thermal lift, but when we find it we should recognize it for what it is and welcome the free lift.

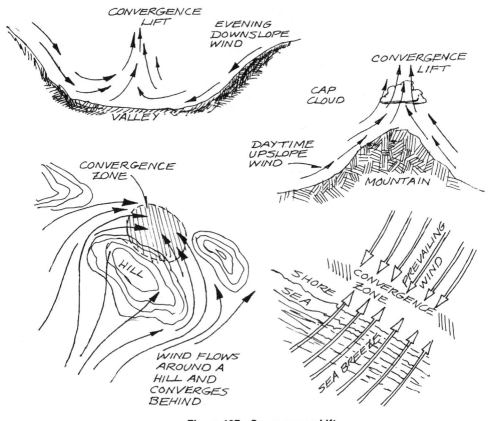

Figure 127 · Convergence Lift

CLEARING YOUR TURNS

The ability to soar brings up the possibility of flying in traffic, for other pilots want to join in the fun. Review and obey the rules of the road outlined in Chapter VII. Besides these rules you need to develop a general see-and-avoid policy. Of utmost importance is to always clear your turns. To do this, look in the direction you are going to turn long before you make the actual control action. Your looking will inform other alert pilots of your intentions as well as let you see if it is clear to turn. Remember, a faster aircraft can come from behind and move to your side to surprise you, so its best to look both ways then continue to look in the direction you are turning as the turn progresses. Clearing turns is a basic practice, but it's amazing how many pilots fail to do so and thus jeopardize their safety and that of others.

Quite often you will experience soaring along side hang glider pilots. They are faster and less maneuverable than you are, so avoid cutting in front of them and watch out for their wake turbulence. They should extend you similar courtesies. Paragliders and hang gliders mix quite nicely in thermals for the faster speeds of the hang glider means they go around you on your paraglider and you can stay on opposite sides of the thermal as you go up together.

In the section on thermal soaring we mentioned circling and figure eight patterns to stay in the best lift of a thermal. For some situations, figure eights may be the most efficient way to work the lift due to the reduction in time you are banked in a turn. It is also easier to avoid being drifted too far behind a mountain when using figure eights. However, using figure eights in traffic is very dangerous for other pilots (whether paragliders or hang gliders) cannot depend on the consistency of your pattern. Hang gliders especially cannot make quick reversing turns so they cannot join a tight figure eight pattern. Circling is the only safe way to work a thermal when other pilots are nearby trying to do the same.

When you enter a thermal that other pilots are working you must be sure to circle in the same direction and intercept the established circle tangent to the circumference rather than aim for the center. Also, when there is traffic around, avoid reversing your circling direction or other pilots will be unable to predict your location. Mass confusion may occur in this case, and you may all go down in a tangled heap.

THUNDERSTORM AVOIDANCE

Thunderstorms are created by essentially the same mechanism as thermals—rising warm air currents. The difference is more humidity which increases the air's bouyancy and cloud buildup. In Chapter IV we covered thunderstorms and their dangers. You should reread this material to refresh your memory.

Here we will mention the escape routes from a thunderstorm. To begin we should understand that such a storm normally develops gradually but at times can build up in fifteen minutes or so. One of the signs of the buildup of a thunderstorm is widespread, often strong, often smooth, lift. This is known in the parlance of pilots as "cloud suck".

Getting sucked up into a cloud, especially if it turns into a thunderstorm, is no fun. To prevent this from happening, be suspicious. Expect cloud suck any time the lift gets widespread or stronger. Look for cloud forming above you. If there is no cloud you're in wave or convergence lift. If you see a cloud building above you, move to an area of safety. This is in front of the lift (upwind) or down to a lower altitude (normally the ground if it's truly a thunderstorm in the making).

Use your well-practiced spiral, turns or full horseshoe stalls to lose altitude the fastest. If you can't escape the lift by diving, you should try to run to the side of it. If you are away from the ridge, go crosswind to escape a thunderstorm as shown in figure 128. If you are on a ridge you may have to penetrate into the wind to get away in order to avoid ridge lift and find a landing field. The worse direction to head is downwind, for it's in this direction that the thunderstorm produces its gust front when it drops rain as shown in the figure. Even if you escape the storm downwind it will soon pass over you.

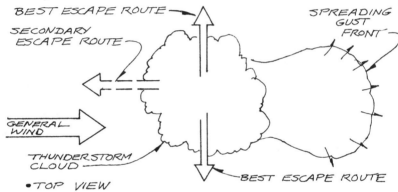

Figure 128 · Escaping a Thunderstorm

It should be clear that thunderstorms and aviation do not get along. A paraglider is a frail vehicle to use for exploring the limits of survival in the atmospheric maelstrom that is a thunderstorm.

Three pilots inflate their canopies. Note possible threat of thunderstorm in background.

AEROMEDICAL CONSIDERATIONS

As you fly higher and longer, you need to understand how your body handles the new situations through which you put it. The first matter will look at is cloud flying.

If you do blunder into a cloud or enter one intentionally, you should know what to expect. Fortunately, due to the extreme stability of our wings, loss of control in a cloud is not a problem (except for in the case of strong turbulence which is sometimes in clouds). However, disorientation can occur rapidly and totally in a cloud. This effect is called *vertigo* and results in nausea and the inability to make proper control decisions.

To avoid vertigo, stay out of clouds or try to maintain a straight course if you do enter one. The worse time is when you just enter or just exit the cloud for you can still see the ground which is moving a different direction than your reference in the cloud.

To relieve yourself from the disorientation of vertigo, focus on a nearby steady object (your feet) or the horizon if you are out of the cloud. You probably will not get rid of any nausea you experience until you land.

Our next consideration is *airsickness*. Yes, this problem occasionally raises its ugly head even when you are having fun. Several things can make this problem worse. Fear and cold or excessive heat can bring on symptoms of nausea and unease. Vertigo can produce sudden nausea. In general, excessive motion due to turbulence or swinging of your head can cause airsickness.

To cure or prevent airsickness, try to focus on distant objects (the horizon) to maintain your sense of balance and keep your turns at a minimum, especially reversing turns. Also, try to breath in a deep regular manner. A series of deep breaths can often allay nausea. Try to dress in clothing that can be opened for ventilation and closed for warmth.

Airsickness is a curious beast in that it can occur in unexpected situations. Don't despair, for you can build up a tolerance to airsickness. Try to figure what caused it besides vigorous turbulence. Was it something you ate? A general unhealthy feeling or attitude? Are you tense?

If all else fails, you can usually cure airsickness with motion sickness drugs. These are a last resort cure and must be tested carefully before you use them in flight. Some of the popular drugs cause drowsiness. Check with your doctor or pharmacist for professional guidance. Remember, you need all your faculties for flying with judgement.

Once we learn to thermal soar we open up the possibility of gaining great altitudes. One problem encountered at heights is *hypoxia* or lowered oxygen in the blood and to the brain. This occurs because the air is thinner at altitude. Most people suffer some effects of hypoxia above 10,000 ft. (3,000m) and it gets progressively worse as altitude is gained.

The symptoms of hypoxia are euphoria, inability to make (wise) decisions, random errors, slurred speech, blue fingernails and a false feeling of well-being. Sounds like a drunk doesn't it? That's exactly what the symptoms initiate, for the cause of the hypoxia symptoms is the same as alcohol drunkeness—lowered oxygen to the brain.

The effects of hypoxia are insidious for you often don't recognize the signs in your euphoric state. The cure is to avoid getting too high and staying too long. Also, cigarettes, coffee and caffeine containing soft drinks render you more susceptible to hypoxia for these drugs constrict the capillaries. This really is only a problem in the western United States where these extreme altitudes can be achieved.

We should make mention here that altitude and the effects of hypoxia will reduce your night vision, so late flights at high altitude sites may compromise safety.

Another short item to consider is the fact that SCUBA diving and high flying do not mix. If you ascend (or even drive to a site) several thousand feet above your dive level, nitrogen disolved in your blood under the pressure of the dive may come out of solution and cause the bends, just as it does if you ascend too quickly during your dive. The safest policy is to wait at least 24 hours before flying after a dive.

The final consideration is your creature comfort. When soaring for long periods of time you must have a comfortable harness to relax and stay loose. Generally, if you are pleasantly dressed on the ground you will be too cool in flight. Remember the wind chill factor of a constant 15 mph breeze in the air. It's perhaps better to be too warm than too cold.

SUMMARY

When you have arrived at this level of achievement you should be capable of passing your Intermediate requirements and some Advanced requirements as well as the Special Skills which include ridge soaring, 360° turns, thermal soaring, cliff or ramp launch, spot landings, high altitude launch and top landing (towing is left for the next chapter). Congratulations.

Now that you have reached this level you must be wary of a problem created by human nature. This problem, contains elements of overconfidence, ego and incomplete understanding. It is generally an attitude whereby the pilot assumes he or she knows about all there is to know and becomes complacent in his or her daily flying.

You should constantly submit yourself to honest self-examination and assess your practices and decisions. Do you fly in high winds or hazardous turbulence? Are you unreceptive to constructive criticism? Do you attempt feats performed by pilots with much more experience? Do these questions bother you?

You must recognize that all of us can suffer from errors of judgement of this sort and we must avoid its dangers by maintaining a conservative attitude towards flying. Risking our lives to impress others does nothing but reflect immaturity. We must learn to work on our skills and judgement gradually and continuously if we want to soar with the eagles.

CHAPTER IX

More Adventures

The joy of flight will always remain with you as long as you find new avenues to explore. There are many facets of paragliding open to the adventurous pilot. Some of these are photography, alpine descent, tandem flying, cross-country flying, competition and towing. We will explore each one in turn so that you can see what's involved and imagine the possibilities. Like all of the subjects in this book, most of these feats require a good understanding and a careful approach to practice them safely. With that admonition, let the fun begin.

AERIAL PHOTOGRAPHY

Taking pictures in the air to show friends and relatives your point of view high above the ground is a lot better idea than boring them with videos of your recent trip to Newark, New Jersey. Some of the shots are bound to be quite fascinating and if you have a special talent, quite aesthetic as well. There's no doubt you can snap some nice panoramas from the air.

The equipment to use is whatever you have handy (part of the challenge is getting your old beater to work for you), although the ideal camera is a modern lightweight 35 mm mechanism. A wide angle lens is preferable in order to take in as much scenery as possible unless you are trying for some special effect. About 35 or 40 mm lens is ideal. Of course your film should be outdoor type unless you fly in enclosed stadiums. The final bit of equipment necessary for anything but point of view shots is a remote shutter control, either electronic or mechanical.

If you are taking any photos other than what your eyes sees—in other words if you want to be in the picture—you must find some way of rigging the camera to your lines or risers. This is not particularly easy to do and is of some concern lest you inadvertently shorten a line or add an imbalance in the system. Naturally, you cannot mount a camera directly to the canopy due to the distortion the extra weight will cause. Perhaps the best solution is to construct a webbing that supports the camera from a number of symmetrically located lines.

When mounting a camera in this manner, be sure to test the system first by inflating the canopy in wind to make sure the glider will stabilize and control normally. Otherwise the only aerial photos you may be able to take will be those of you crashing on launch.

CLIMBING AND DESCENT

As gratifying as mountain climbing is in itself, there is a certain enhancement to the whole prospect of climbing a majestic peak when you know you can glide down from it. Paragliders have descended in this manner from over 25,000 feet (8,000 m). This is a popular pastime and deserves a bit of mention.

To begin, the equipment in use for this practice is both standard paragliders and specially made gear for extreme light weight. A "descent" glider is often smaller than a standard glider and may weigh as much as four pounds (2 kg) less. Of course, flying speeds will be faster, but the object is not necessarily to soar from the high peaks.

A word of caution is appropriate here. Higher mountains can exhibit much higher winds than we are used to in the lower hill country. These winds can also be extremely turbulent, especially in areas that are surrounded by desert conditions. Mountain flights can be treacherous for any form of aviation in some conditions. The reader should also consider the effects of altitude on takeoff speed (remember that little canopy). Certainly a bit of headwind at takeoff is desirable. Perhaps the only safe policy is to always plan to hike down the mountain rather than fly so if conditions don't look good at the top you can keep your glider packed and live to come back another day. Remember, on the scale of human existence, the mountains will always be there.

Paragliding combines nicely with hiking, climbing and other modes of travel.

FLYING AROUND

One of the very attractive things about a paraglider is the fact that it is the world's most lightweight and compact aircraft. This makes it ideal for travel. Flying other sites in other parts of the country or other countries themselves is great fun. You meet many other pilots, expand your experience level and get some exotic stories to tell back home.

When you go to a new place to fly, don't forget site protocol. Many sites have reasonable rules to follow and you sure don't want to wear out your welcome. The local pilots are also the best source of information as to how their hill should be flown to maximize enjoyment. They can tell you where the "house thermal" resides and where the turbulence lurks as well as how low you can go and still reach a landing field.

You should be aware that different conditions exist in different areas. The most obvious differences are the ground cover. In the eastern US, trees abound and it is hard indeed to find an abundance of good paragliding sites. Ski areas are the best bet here if they will grant you permission (many won't due to liability). In the western US, England, and Europe there are many bare hills and alpine pastures that accomodate paraglider launches nicely.

Less obvious than the ground cover are the weather differences. The western areas of the US are noted for dry conditions with light upper winds, often strong upslope winds and strong thermals. The eastern US, England and Europe experience more frontal passage that brings changing conditions and also much more laminar airflow that can result in penetration problems. Also, because these areas are more moist they naturally exhibit more gentle thermals with less turbulence. Each area obviously has its own problems to solve and unique features that are part of the attraction of flying new sites.

TANDEM FLYING

Flying with two on one wing can be very enjoyable for you get to share the view and excitement. It's also a great teaching device in the hands of a competent instructor. However, there are many dangers involved that must be understood.

To begin, a tandem pilot must be certified as such by the APA through an exemption from the FAA in the US. What all this alphabet soup means is that those in the know recognize the dangers tandem flying can pose to those

A tandem launch in the high mountains.

163

not prepared to handle the greater difficulties. Also, unsuspecting passengers are somewhat protected if the pilot has had some formal training.

The dangers of tandem flying are higher speeds due to the additional loading and less control due to the larger canopies used. A final danger is the lack of coordination between pilot and passenger that can lead to the passenger tripping and a hard mutual fall.

The equipment necessary for a tandem flight is a larger glider and a special harness. Canopies from 300 to 325 square feet (32 to 35 square meters) are the minimum that should be used. Even at those sizes the wing loading is increased as much as 60% resulting in takeoff speeds 25% greater than in a single-place canopy. The harness is specially built with the risers routed from the pilot in the rear, through the harness of the passenger in front and backup as in figure 129. The other special equipment item is a helmet with a full face mask for the pilot to prevent injury to him if the passenger jumps up on takeoff or stops abruptly on landing.

Before a flight takes place the passenger must be carefully briefed. He must know the signals (ready canopy, lift and clear) and practice running with the instructor. During takeoff the passenger grasps his harness and

PASSENGER KEEPS ARMS CLEAR OF RISERS AND CONTROLS.

NOTE FULL FACE HELMET

PILOT POSITIONED ABOVE AND BEHIND THE PASSENGER.

Figure 129 · Tandem Flying

doesn't let go until the pilot tells him. The passenger runs without stopping upon the clear command.

Tandem flying should never take place without a full assist crew. This means at least two canopy men and a harness man. There must always be a headwind present to aid the takeoff or the situation is too critical and unsafe. There is little room for error in such a situation, so the canopy must be well stabilized overhead before takeoff is attempted.

Because the pilot is normally behind and hung slightly above the passenger (about 1 foot), he will be in the air first on takeoff. For that reason the passenger must continue running on the clear command. Once in the air the situation and control is not a problem and feels like a normal flight except for higher speeds.

Before landing the passenger must be prepared by having him regrasp his harness. The student must be cautioned to avoid pulling down on the risers. The landing itself must be performed by the pilot from the passenger's point of view. That is, the flare occurs when the passenger is the right height, not the pilot. Needless to say, the pilot must have consummate landing skills to do this safely. The passenger must be instructed not to fall down for if he does he pulls the pilot down on top of him and who's to know who will get hurt during the entanglement. The passenger should also be instructed to keep his feet together and knees bent to prevent tripping (assuming the pilot performs a perfect crisp flare!).

From the foregoing it should be obvious that tandem flying is not as simple as stepping off alone. However, with proper training from the APA a pilot can learn to fly tandem safely and share the joy of simple flight.

CROSS-COUNTRY FLYING

Cruising the countryside from on high is a wonderful image, but cross-country flying usually entails lots of concentration, lots of decision making and little time for sight-seeing. No matter, it's still marvelous fun and very rewarding. The first time you rack up miles in your paraglider, you'll land with a great feeling of accomplishment.

To fly cross-country you must use every bit of lift you find along the way to gain height. This means putting yourself in the best position to find lift at all times. Obviously, flying along a mountain chain or ridge is the best choice of routes, both to find ridge lift and thermals. Over flat country you must position yourself over areas likely to produce thermals. Review the material on thermals to understand this.

The best way to cover the maximum distance is to fly with the wind (in the downwind direction). The problem with that is you must go over at least the mountain from which you launched. A general rule of thumb here is:

> •Never go over a mountain with less than the height of the mountain above it.

This policy assures that you will have enough altitude to travel far enough to avoid rotors and turbulence on the mountain's downwind side. In figure 130 we see this illustrated. If you do pass over such a mountain, be sure to fly downwind as far as you can. After all, the idea is to add on miles.

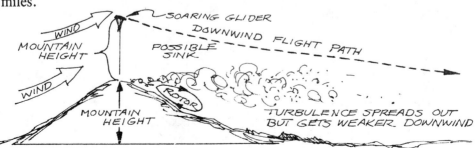

Figure 130 · Flying Over a Mountain

165

Of course, heading directly downwind may not be possible if landing fields aren't available or lift sources look scarce. In any case, you must use all your knowledge to determine the best route as you encounter new conditions. It helps if you pore over maps to check out routes.

Driving along a chosen route can show you where the safe landing fields and nasty items like power lines are. Every time you fly you can try ranging out a little further until finally you catch the big one that lets you break away. Go with it, but remember that for the fun to continue, a safe flight must ensue.

COMPETITION

Most sports eventually develop some sort of competition as participants improve their skills and wish to compare them with others and seek greater challenges. Paragliding is no exception. The form this competition takes is limited only by the imagination of the meet organizers.

Duration (time aloft) and spot landing contests are two traditional favorites (often combined) that are good spectator sports. To maximize your duration you must fly at minimum sink while in zero or lifting air and faster to quickly find more lift when you fall into sinking air. Of course, if the air isn't varying, you maintain minimum sink. In this task, the larger the canopy (the lower your wing loading) the slower you will sink.

We briefly covered spot landings in Chapter VI. Here we'll add the suggestion that you practice spots assiduously in all types of conditions in order to perfect your judgement. Whichever landing set-up you use (aircraft approach, figure eights or a combination), concentrate on your spot and try to keep the same general pattern every time.

A special type of spot landing is a touch-and-go on the side of a hill. In this practice you must maintain precise control and approach across the hill. Because of the difference in judgement required compared to spot landing, side hill touch-and-goes demand much practice on their own.

Competitors line up at the 1989 World Meet in Kossen, Austria.

Another typical task is maneuvers around pylons. This may involve figure eights or some other pattern to test your maneuvering skills. This is where all your practice at controlling your ground track pays off. You must make your turns precise and efficient to conserve altitude and complete the tasks.

Other pylon courses may be actual cross-country tasks requiring you to gain altitude in order to reach a goal or a series of pylons. Here you call on your previous cross-country experience to provide judgement and skill for finding the right air to take you further.

Next we have named duration events. In this case you declare the amount of time you will be in the air and try to touch down precisely when this time elapses. You must be very familiar with your canopy's performance to be successful here. Again, practice is the secret.

Altitude gain and bomb drops are two more fun events. In the latter case you try to drop a flour bag or other soft weight onto a target from a minimum altitude. This requires real talent, for your forward motion compticates the bomb's trajectory. Try it, but make sure a wide area is clear below.

Finally, we should mention prescribed maneuvers and aerial ballet. In this event you are required to perform certain maneuvers such as three consecutive spiral turns, roll out on a predetermined heading, crab along a predetermined ground track, make a series of linked turns at full brakes then repeat at half brakes, perform a downwind base and final, then land. This all may be timed with any combination of turns required. Your scoring may be on the basis of the cleanliness of your maneuvers and a point system relating to the control of your ground track or both.

Serious competition is not for everyone, of course. For those pilots bored with taking sled rides and dead-wind glides at their home sites, here's a fun wrinkle: tether a helium filled balloon a hundred or so feet off the ground with a light thread. Try to fly down and kick it with one foot as you pass. You'll be amazed at how this hones your three-dimensional spatial judgement. Be cautious of stalling in this game, however. A safety feature is to declare that all pilots using more than half brakes receive a zero score.

HILL CLIMBING ASSIST

With sufficient wind you can use your glider to help you climb a hill for a flight down. This requires almost 10 mph (16 km/h) wind but shouldn't be practiced in winds much over 15 mph if you don't want to go for a drag.

The technique consists of performing a reverse inflation and playing with the brakes to produce extra lift as you moon-walk up the hill. Sometimes you can take great leaps, but be cautious of getting airborne. In any case you should be prepared to fly with helmet on and harness fully attached in case you get surprised by a gust.

Remember, close to the terrain the wind is usually variable so you may have to continually control the glider with risers and brakes (remember the "box" pattern described in Chapter VI). Also, be prepared to collapse the canopy immediately and run towards it if things get out of hand. When the canopy crests the top of a hill it can encounter stronger winds, so be especially vigilent here to avoid getting dragged over the top. Keep on your feet!

TETHERED FLIGHT

One of the easiest ways for a beginner to learn to inflate and control a paraglider is to be tethered. This practice involves tying the pilot off to ropes so he can ascend in a wind like a kite. In order for tethering to be done safely, a few rules must be observed.

To begin, the wind must be greater than the glider's stall speed. Between 10 and 15 mph (16 to 24 km/h) wind on the ground is about right. Remember, the wind will be stronger as we ascend due to wind gradient. With these wind speeds, a steady wind is necessary or the glider will oscillate and possibly lock out or collapse. As in many flying situations, conditions are the critical matter.

The second matter to consider is the tetherline. Strength is not a major concern here, but line arrangement is. A pilot should never be tethered with a single line. The reason for this is the danger of a lockout (see the next section for a discussion of lockouts). Just like a kite can dive to the ground, so can a glider when tethered. The cure and prevention to this dangerous phenomenon is to use two tether lines as shown in figure 131. These lines should be angled outward from the body of the pilot as shown.

The two tether line should be attached to the pilot's harness at separate points on either side of the harness to afford stability (attaching the lines at the same point on the harness is not the cure for lockouts). Generally, a quick release system is not used when tethering since it is difficult to release both lines at once. Carabiners or quick links can be used to fasten the ropes to the harness.

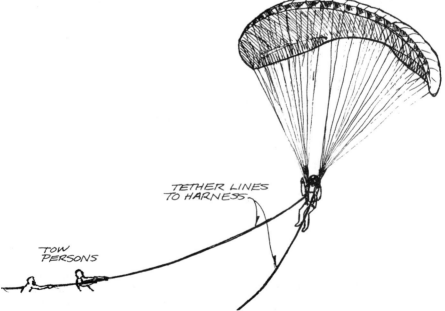

TETHER LINES
TO HARNESS

TOW
PERSONS

Figure 131 - Tethering A Paraglider

168

The other ends of the tether lines should be held by tow persons (not tied to a fixed anchor point). This allows for a limit to the tow force as well as the possibility of release. Knots or loops in the lines will assist the tow persons in holding the line, but they should be of the proper size to allow easy release.

When flying under tether, the pilot inflates the canopy as usual, but a non-reversing inflation is used despite the wind. The tether lines should be taut to prevent the pilot from dragging backwards. As soon as inflation is complete and the canopy is checked the tow persons can begin pulling to add a little lift to the canopy. Generally, as the pilot rises higher the increased wind eliminates the need to run the tether lines.

Once the pilot is aloft he or she can practice brake control by starting with brakes at 50% then apply less and more brakes to experience the effects. This practice is a good teaching technique and some schools use tethering as a means of introducing beginning pilots to flight.

Pilots should be cautioned to avoid making dramatic turn controls when tethered for turning the canopy in relation to the tether lines can lead to a lockout. In the next section we tow with only one line. However, a maximum tension reel, weak links and quick releases are the safety factors in this situation. Remember to tether in smooth conditions and the results will be instructive and fun.

TOWING

Flat landers have always had trouble practicing foot launch flying. But being the avid pilots that they are, they create artificial mountains by towing aloft. Towing has some advantages over mountain flying, namely that you don't have to drive up rugged mountains, but there are some drawbacks too. You have to have a properly set up tow rig, a well maintained tow site and adequate training. The latter point is important, for towing adds complications to paragliding that can turn into dangers if they get out of hand. This material is meant to be an introduction to towing, not a complete manual. Any reader contemplating the towing of a paraglider is urged to take lessons or get guidance from experienced pilots. The APA can help you with names and location of towing activity.

TOWING TYPES

We will distinguish two major types of towing: static line and winch. A static line tow consists of a given length of line attached to the back of a vehicle on one end and hooked to the pilot on the other end. A winch tow consists of a reel that pays out as the pilot gets higher. These systems can be on the back of a truck or boat. Note that sailplane-type towing whereby a winch reels in line to pull the glider aloft must not be used for these winches generally cannot quickly relieve line tension in case of an emergency.

EQUIPMENT

The most critical part of your equipment is naturally your paraglider. You must have a canopy built to withstand the extra forces induced by towing. Note that these forces may cause stretch in a normal canopy.

Check with your manufacturer to see if you can tow yours safely.

Next, you must have a tow line set up. This consists of a length of rope, a drogue parachute and releases at both ends. The line itself should be 3/8″ polypropylene. The choice of this line is due to its lightness, strength and low cost. Don't be tempted to use stouter line, for your canopy has to lift the weight of the rope (as well as you) and rope breaking can be a safety valve for high tow forces. The length of rope you use is up to you within certain limits. The minimum length is about 300 feet (90m) so that you have time to recover after you release. The maximum length is about 2000 feet (600m). Any longer than this and the driver cannot see the pilot's signals adequately.

The releases at the ends of the rope are for safety if an emergency should occur. At the pilot end a Y is spliced into the line so that the line can connect to either side of the pilot's harness. Quick links allow for easy attachment. At the apex of this Y there is a quick release as shown in figure 132. This release must be padded so that it doesn't injure the pilot if it springs back when it is deployed or the line breaks. There is at least one pilot who lost an eye in this manner.

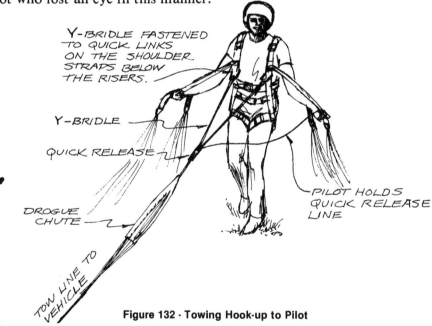

Y-BRIDLE FASTENED TO QUICK LINKS ON THE SHOULDER STRAPS BELOW THE RISERS.

Y-BRIDLE

QUICK RELEASE

DROGUE CHUTE

PILOT HOLDS QUICK RELEASE LINE

TOW LINE TO VEHICLE

Figure 132 - Towing Hook-up to Pilot

Also pictured in the figure is a drogue chute that inflates when tension is off the line and helps prevent the line from snapping back at the tow vehicle as well as dropping the line progressively in a straight line. Note the quick release cord to the yoke also shown in the figure.

The release at the vehicle end of the rope is similar to that at the pilot end. The best release to use in either case is a "three ring circus" which is a series of interlocking rings that release with very little force and have a low probability of malfunctioning. An additional quick release is often placed where the rope attaches to the vehicle so the line can be released for the vehicle to drive to the other end and pull it back to the staging ground.

This release should be a sailplane type for quick usage.

A weak link should be used in the tow line near the pilot release. This weak link is designed to break in case the tow forces get too high and the pilot doesn't have time to release. A wear link breaking at about 200 lbs (90 kg) should be sufficient. You must expirement to find the proper weak link for your operation. Be sure to err on the side of weakness when you begin this test.

You can make a weak link by using Dacron chord wrapped around a pair of rings. The more wraps you use, the stronger the weak link. Test the link by hanging it up and adding weight to it. Remember to protect the weak link from abrasion or it will quickly weaken when you haul in the line.

A very important piece of equipment is a tensiometer. This device allows the driver to monitor the line tension at all times and prevent towing with too great a force.

CAUTION: Any towing of a "square" canopy or paraglider that takes place over land must employ a tensiometer or a weak link in the line to prevent "overtowing."

Winches used for towing consist of large drums with a braking mechanism and a method of reeling back the line. Such a winch is costly, but allows the line to be pulled in efficiently and allows the pilot to take off near the vehicle, for the line pays out as the pilot climbs.

Radios with voice actuated microphones are ideal communication devices for towing (obviously they can't be used for water operations). To use them effectively, however, a few brief signals must be employed so immediate action is taken in an emergency.

The tow vehicles themselves demand some attention as they are the biggest investment involved. If you are water towing you need a special boat. A deep V hull is required for directional stability. Also a minimum of 115 horsepower is required. The ideal boat is a jet-boat because the engine doesn't stick up in back. You must have a good tow line anchor on the boat—ski pylons are not necessarily strong enough. Note: if you are towing over water, you must use a water repellent canopy for if the canopy gets wet unevenly it may display a wicked turn.

A vehicle used for land towing must have a 360° view for the driver. Pickup trucks or dune buggies qualify, but vans or cars must not be used. The driver controls the safety of the situation and must monitor the pilot at all times.

LINE CARE

Taking good care of your line will make it retain its strength longer which is an economic as well as safety factor. Don't run over it with your vehicle and don't drag it on the ground any faster than 10 mph (16 km/h). Be careful of catching it on a wheel and winding it on an axle. If your line does break, splice it together, do not knot it. Knots can bind in a winch and weaken a rope from 40 to 60%. Breaks are likely to happen when you are towing the rope back to the staging area and it hooks on something. If it does snag, do not pull it with the vehicle, but pull it clear by hand. Always check your line on the drive back to its pilot end and when you reel it in. Catching and removing weak sections can help prevent stressful in-air line breaks.

When you put your rope away at night, the best method is to store it loose in a drum, or chain link it. This allows the polypropylene rope to relax and thus extends its life. This is one problem with winches, for the rope is often wound up under tension.

THE DRIVER AND PILOT

As mentioned, the driver is the key individual in the towing operation. He is in charge of all phases of the flight until the pilot releases. He responds to the pilot's signaled requests and the visual clues of line tension and pilot position in relation to the canopy.

The driver is responsible for connecting the towline to the pilot and the truck. Too many people involved with the operation can cause confusion and errors. The only exception to this is the use of a signal person stationed next to the pilot to communicate with the driver. A trained signal person can serve to aid the pilot in hook-up and positioning.

The driver should not allow anyone to be in the truck (except an instructor in the training situation) to avoid distraction and accidents if he has to brake suddenly. Since the driver must watch the pilot, he must clear the runout area of spectators, animals, debris and terrain irregularities. One driver who failed to do this found himself straddling a gulley while the pilot sailed silently over his head.

The driver should understand the situation from the pilot's end so anyone driving a tow vehicle should know how to fly. Of course, the driver must be very versed in the standard signals.

The pilot is at the mercy of the driver for the most part so the driver must be trained in the proper use of signals and emergency procedures as well as be experienced in normal takeoff and flying control. The only exception to this is a training situation under the close guidance of an experienced instructor.

TAKEOFF PROCEDURES

Once the line is layed out properly and the canopy positioned for launch (the same as a normal assisted or unassisted takeoff), the truck and pilot take their positions and hook into the line. Wind socks should be placed at both ends of the field for proper wind assessment. If conditions are good, the operation proceeds. If not, a stand down order is given.

When the pilot is ready, the signal is given for the truck to take up the rope slack. This must be done very slowly. As the rope tension begins pulling at the pilot, he lets it build by holding his ground then he signals his wing assistants to lift the canopy (unless unassisted) and performs the normal takeoff procedure.

The driver continues to take up rope slack (unless a stop signal is given) and accelerates to initial tension as soon as the canopy is over the pilot's head and in good shape (no end cell closure). At this point the driver watches the tensiometer, pilot and canopy with great care. If the pilot falls or signals to stop, this must be done immediately with a hard braking action. In normal conditions with light wind and a steady pull, the pilot should be off the ground in two to three paces and must not jump. Figure 133 illustrates a normal lift-off.

Once the canopy is in the air the pilot must hold it straight with the steering lines. He or she must stay directly behind the truck. As the vehicle begins to increase the tension immediately after lift off, the pilot should apply half brakes to increase the lifting action.

If no wind is present, the driver must increase speed slightly (and thus tension) as lift-off occurs. If wind is present, little additional speed beyond that required to take up slack may be needed. In a crosswind, the pilot may have to run left or right a little to compensate. The steering should also be used to keep the canopy into the wind if it is crossing. Also, the canopy may be laid out angled a bit into the wind. At most, a 30° crossing wind can be tolerated.

Here's a *PRO-TIP*: "The art of good towing is keeping a smooth and consistant tension in the line and not overtowing".

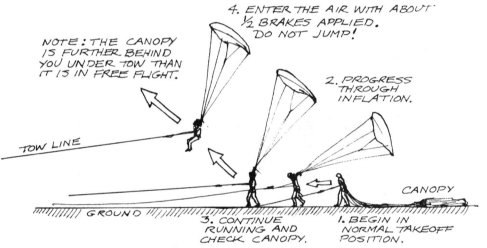

Figure 133 · Normal Towing Lift-off

SIGNALS

There are standard signals that should be used in all towing operations. These are necessary because the driver and pilot are separated by more than a third of a mile on a long line. Even when using radios these signals must be understood in case of a radio malfunction.

The takeoff signals may be given by a signal person. The standard signals are shown in figure 134. Note the use of fluorescent paddles for visibility. The *take up slack* signal is in reality the indication that all is ready and launch should proceed. Note that the driver can choose to ignore this "go" signal if something is wrong from his viewpoint. If the pilot is alone, the signal to take up slack and proceed through takeoff is jumping up and down—a curious but effective signal. To tell the driver to stop, the pilot spreads his or her legs.

In-air signals are given by the pilot only and consist of a signal to the driver to *slow down* by opening and closing the legs rapidly as shown in figure 135. The signal to *speed up* is flapping the arms up and down like a bird as shown in the figure. Finally, the emergency *stop and release* tension signal is to hold the legs open wide as shown. This last signal should elicit an immediate and deliberate response. The first two signals are requests, the last one a demand.

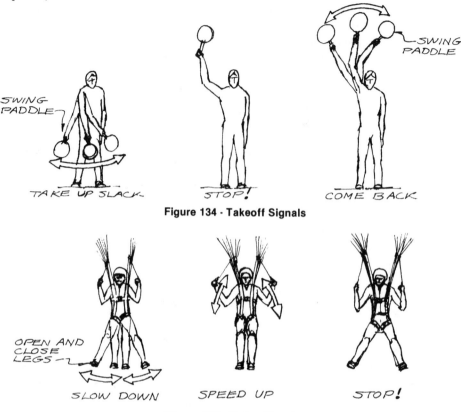

Figure 134 · Takeoff Signals

Figure 135 · Flying Signals

FLYING ON TOW

The tow vehicle is the engine of the wing at the end of the tow line. The driver must control this engine wisely. The control information is line tension, not vehicle speed, for in varying winds the force on the line will be greatly altered if ground speed is the same. It should be clear that towing should not take place in gusty conditions for the driver can't adjust speed fast enough to even out the line tensions unless a very responsive winch is employed

Once the canopy inflates and is clear, the tow proceeds slowly and steadily. It is important that the pilot is off the ground quickly and not running along the field. Initially the tow tensions should be light—less than 250 pounds (113 kg). Maintain this light pressure until 100 feet (30 m), then gradually increase tension to a maximum of 400 pounds (180 kg). The tow forces are kept light at the lower altitude to reduce the chance of a line break which is more serious close to the ground.

During climbout, the pilot must always fly behind the vehicle and not oscillate. Oscillation in a square canopy is a sign of overtowing (too fast). If the vehicle must turn, the pilot should always remain over the vehicle's track (on land) or wake (over water) and not turn directly when the vehicle does.

As the canopy climbs, the driver must be aware of the possibility for higher winds aloft and monitor the tensiometer. The pilot will climb to about a 60° angle to the ground as shown in figure 136. Increasing the tow tension to get the pilot higher is risky as it puts too much load on the

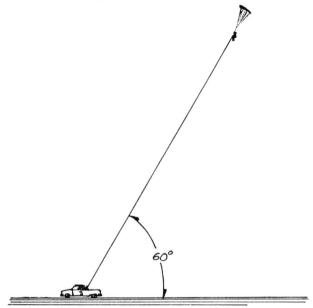

Figure 136 · Normal Maximum Tow Position

glider. When towing round canopies (including a Paracommander), a good rule of thumb is to adjust towing speed until the pilot's head just touches the rear of the canopy, according to the drivers line of sight. This is shown in figure 137. It bears repeating that the driver must constantly watch the attitude of the canopy and the pilot for signals.

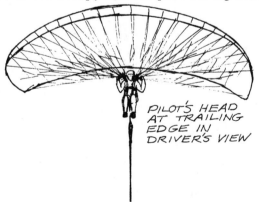

PILOT'S HEAD AT TRAILING EDGE IN DRIVER'S VIEW

Figure 137 · Proper Tow Position

RELEASING FROM TOW

Once the maximum height is gained or the driver runs out of room, it's time to come off tow. The pilot can signal the driver to stop and the line will slacken. It's important to realize that the tow line adds energy to the glider and it is not flying at the normal attitude. This is shown in figure 138. Consequently, the nose of the glider must be lowered (or will lower itself) as the line is released. If the tension is not relieved by the vehicle stopping, the results of the release will be dramatic (see tow line brakes below).

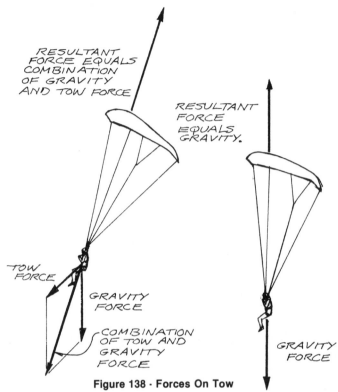

Figure 138 · Forces On Tow

Once the line is slack the pilot should pull his release and fly free from the earthly bonds. The driver then retrieves the line. Note that if you operate in a crosswind the drogue chute will drift the line across your field. Make sure it doesn't fall on powerlines, trees or houses. It may be hard to retrieve in these instances. The driver releases the line at his end (assuming a static line) and pulls it back from the other end or reels it in if a winch is used.

CAUTION: Children are fascinated by the towing operation and have a tendency to stand on the line or grab it in play. The consequences if you are dragging the line are burned hands or feet!

EMERGENCY PROCEDURES

There are two common enough emergencies that all towing operations should know how to handle. The first is a line break and the second is a lockout.

Line breaks shouldn't happen if you maintain your tow rope properly, use reasonable tow forces and avoid gusty conditions. But if they do occur, they are not too problematic if ample altitude is available.

176

When a line breaks, the pilot will swing back and the canopy will dive forward because of the sudden reduction of the forward pull on the pilot (see figure 138). The pilot should react by immediately applying ½ brakes to slow the canopy before a dive ensues. The pilot will then swing back to the normal position and the canopy will stabilize.

Once stabilized, the pilot should release the portion of the line still attached to his bridle. Dragging the line is very dangerous for it can snag on the ground and cause severe circumstances as you can well imagine. Then the pilot must assess the landing zone and his altitude. If altitude is minimal, he should apply a vigorous flare just before reaching the ground and perform a parachute landing roll (see Chapter VI). Remember:

> **Line Breaks**
> CAUSES: 1. Knots in a line. 2. Old or worn line. 3. Gusty winds. 4. Over-towing.
> PROCEDURES: 1. Apply and hold ½ brakes. 2. Release any remaining line. 3. Locate and perform an emergency landing.

Lockouts are a bit more dangerous and are a result of an inexperienced pilot tugging on a control, overtowing or variable conditions including gusts and wind shear. Ninety percent of lockouts occur due to the latter two factors.

A lockout results when a canopy gets tilted to one side. The tow force combines with the wing forces to pull the canopy further to the side in a quickly escalating tug of war that ends up with the canopy rapidly diving earthward (see figure 139). If you've ever had a string kite swing to one side then barrel into the ground, you've witnessed a lockout.

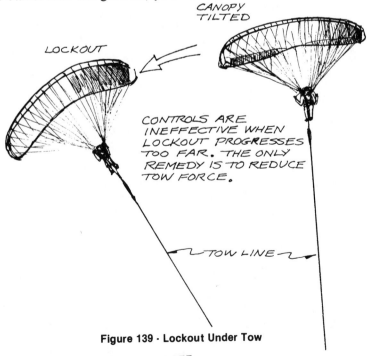

CANOPY TILTED

LOCKOUT

CONTROLS ARE INEFFECTIVE WHEN LOCKOUT PROGRESSES TOO FAR. THE ONLY REMEDY IS TO REDUCE TOW FORCE.

TOW LINE

Figure 139 · Lockout Under Tow

If a glider gets turned to one side during tow, the pilot can often correct. However, after some point the controls are ineffective and a lockout will result. This is a severe emergency and the driver must be alert to take immediate action.

The necessary thing to occur to stop a lockout from continuing to dire circumstances is an immediate relief of line tension. Tow line forces build up rapidly in a lockout so the vehicle must stop and *back up* immediately or turn 180° and drive to the pilot. Remember, a line under tension stretches so the forces are not eliminated by merely stopping.

Once the rope is slackened through the radical maneuvers on the part of the driver, the pilot should release. He most likely will be pointing at the ground in a bank and dive, so application of half brakes is called for. If the driver does not react in time, the pilot must pull his release despite the high forces. The glider will react as with a line, break only more severely. For this reason, the pilot should hold down the brake on the upward side (probably already applied to correct the lockout) and release with the other hand. The release line should always be held in the pilot's hand during tow for just such a contingency. A three ring circus should be employed here for it will release under unlimited tension whereas other releases may jam if the forces are too great.

Once the pilot recovers he should locate a safe landing area and perform a good touch down. Remember:

Lockouts Lore

CAUSES: 1. Inexperienced pilot. 2. Overtowing. 3. Variable conditions.

PROCEDURES: 1. Vehicle stops and backs up. 2. Or vehicle turns and drives to pilot. 3. Release line.

These emergencies are rare or non-existant if the towing operation is performed with care, with safety and with trained individuals. The possibility of gaining great altitude by using thermals off of tow makes this an ideal way for those with horizontal horizons to get a piece of the sky.

THE FUTURE

In this chapter we have explored some of the adjuncts to our sport that add interest and adventure. As we continue our exploration we may develop new forms of flying with our membrane wings. Certainly the cross-country and altitude records will continue to expand and competition will change in format to accomodate ever increasing pilot skills. What passes today for advanced skills will eventually be considered inadequate for an experienced pilot as we learn more about technique and designs become more sophisticated.

However, one thing is certain: we will not stray too far from the concept of simple and convenient flight for that is what attracts us to the sport in the first place. If we constantly maintain our vigilance on that trio of all important items: the wing, the wind and the windividual, we will continue to enjoy our place in the sky and be welcome in the world of aviation. We believe that all humanity deserves the freedom to spread their wings.

A perfect launch ends a perfect day.

APPENDIX I

PILOT PROFICIENCY PROGRAM

APA pilot ratings are issued to reflect completion of WITNESSED tasks to demonstrate a level of skill necessary to fly a paraglider. Four levels of skill are recognized including a Beginner level, a Novice level, a Intermediate level and a Advanced level of skill. This rating system parallels the United States Hang Gliding Association Pilot Proficiency Program.

Beginner Rating—Required Witnessed Tasks
1. Demonstrates layout and preflight of paraglider and harness, to include familiarity with owner's manual(s).
2. Demonstrates proper ground handling of equipment in winds up to 10 mph.
3. Gives verbal analysis of general conditions of site including ground crew briefing, assisted launch, flight path, flight plan, areas to avoid in relation to wind flow and obstacles to stay clear of, primary and secondary landing zones.
4. With each flight, demonstrates method of establishing that pilot is hooked into and holding the risers properly prior to launch.
5. Launch unassisted showing:
   a) Aggressive run.
   b) Good canopy inflation and control.
   c) Smooth transition from running to flying.
6. Airspeed—Rate of Descent recognition and control.
   a) Two flights, predetermined to show:
      1. Constant airspeed and rate of descent.
      2. Smooth straight flight.
      3. Safe, smooth landing, on feet into wind.
   b) Two flights, predetermined to show:
      1. Confident, slight variation in airspeed and rate of descent showing awareness and control of airspeed envelope.
      2. Smoothly increasing airspeed, smoothly slowing airspeed showing good control, familiarity, and anticipation of safe envelope, without loosing control. Airspeed to remain well above stall speed.
      3. Safe, smooth landing, on feet, into wind.
7. Shows ability to recognize and understand how different wind conditions at the site will affect their flights.
   a) Wind direction.
   b) Wind velocity.
   c) Terrain shape.
   d) Obstructions.
8. On each flight, demonstrates proper post landing procedure, to include but not limited to:
   a) Unhooking, braiding lines.
   b) Checking traffic, Hang Gliders and Paragliders.
   c) Removal of glider from landing area.
   d) Proper packing procedure.
   e) Any specific protocol at this site.
9. Understand APA accident reporting procedures and documentation.
10. Must pass APA Beginner Oral Exam.

Novice Rating—Required Witnessed Tasks
The pilot shall use good judgement and have a level of maturity commensurate with the rating. Pilots must demonstrate beginner level skills and knowledge before obtaining a Novice rating. All witnessed flights must be pre-planned by pilot and discussed with Instructor or Observer.

1. Demonstrates set up and preflight of paraglider and harness including reserve parachute.

2. Demonstrates proper ground handling of equipment in winds up to 15 mph.
3. Gives verbal analysis of general conditions of site including ground crew briefing, assisted launch, flight path, flight plan, areas to avoid in relation to wind flow and obstacles to stay clear of, primary and secondary landing zones.
4. With each flight, demonstrates method of establishing that pilot is hooked into risers properly prior to launch.
5. Launch unassisted showing:
   a) Aggressive run.
   b) Good canopy inflation and control.
   c) Smooth transition from running to flying.
6. Airspeed—Rate of Descent recognition and control.
   a) Two flights, predetermined to show:
      1. Constant airspeed and rate of descent.
      2. Smooth straight flight.
      3. Safe, smooth landing, on feet into wind.
   b) Two flights, predetermined to show:
      1. Confident, slight variation in airspeed and rate of descent showing awareness and control of airspeed envelope.
      2. Smoothly increasing airspeed, smoothly slowing airspeed showing good control, familiarity, and anticipation of safe envelope, without loosing control. Airspeed to remain well above stall speed.
      3. Safe, smootth landing, on feet, into wind.
7. Demonstrates flight(s) along a planned path alternating "S" turns of at least 90 degrees in heading. Flight heading need not exceed 45 degrees from straight into wind. Turns must be smooth with controlled airspeed, ending in safe, stand up landings into the wind.
8. Demonstrate one flight along a planned path alternating "S" turns of at least 180 degrees in heading. Flight heading need not exceed 90 degrees from straight into wind. Turns must be smooth with controlled airspeed, ending in safe, stand up landings into the wind.
9. Demonstrate one smooth, coordinated 360 degree turn.
10. Demonstrates two no-wind launches, two moderate-wind launches, two high-wind launches (10-15 mph), including two reverse launches.
11. Demonstrates two cross wind launches approximately 30 degrees off wind line.
12. Demonstrates three consecutive landings within 100 feet of a target, safe, smooth on feet and into the wind. Turns are required to set up an approach and avoid overflying the target.
13. Demonstrates hands off flying, front riser use, and mild stall and recovery (above 500) demonstrating appropriate limitation of technique.
14. Demonstrates standard aircraft landing approach: downwind, base, and final (winds <10 mph).
15. Demonstrates proper strong wind landing procedures and how to keep from getting dragged back.
16. Shows ability to recognize and understand how different wind conditions at the site will affect their flights.
   a) Wind direction.
   b) Wind velocity.
   c) Terrain shape.
   d) Obstructions.
17. On each flight, demonstrates proper post landing procedure, to include but not limited to:
   a) Unhooking, braiding lines.
   b) Checking traffic, Hang Gliders and Paragliders.
   c) Removal of glider from landing area.
   d) Proper packing procedure.
   e) Any specific protocol at this site.
18. Understand APA accident reporting procedures and documentation.
19. Understand FAR 103.

20. Understand pilot skills necessary for APA "Special Skills."
21. Must pass APA Novice Oral Exam.

Intermediate Rating—Required Witnessed Tasks
   The pilot shall use good judgement and have a level of maturity commensurate with the rating.
1. Must have held a Novice rating for at least four months.
2. Must have logged at least 30 flying days.
3. Must have logged a total of at least 90 flights.
4. Must have logged a minimum of two hours of air time.
5. Has received and understands the importance and or significance of;
    a) Right of Way Rules.
    b) FAA Regulations, sectional charts.
    c) Airspeed control, stalls, spins, canopy collapse.
    d) Glider owner's manual.
    e) APA accident report results currently in print.
6. Can give verbal analysis of conditions on the hill demonstrating knowledge of wind shadows, gradients, lift, sink, laminar air, turbulence and rotors and the effect these items can have on intended flight path and turns.
7. Must give verbal flight plan for each observed flight.
8. Must show thorough preflight of harness and glider, and a reserve parachute.
9. With each flight, demonstrates method of establishing that pilot is hooked into risers properly prior to launch.
10. All takeoffs should be aggressive, confident and with a smooth transition from running to flying. Flights with slow, unstable launches will not be considered adquate as witnessed tasks.
11. For witnessed tasks, all landings must be safe, smooth, on the feet, and in control.
12. Demonstrates the ability to differentiate airspeed from groundspeed.
13. Demonstrates linked 180 degree turns along a predetermined ground track showing smooth controlled reversals and proper coordination at various speeds and angles of bank.
14. Explains stall warning characteristics.
15. Has practiced and demonstrates hands off flying, front riser use, gentle stalls and proper recovery under the direct supervision of an Instructor or qualified Observer, at least 500 feet from any object.
16. Demonstrates smooth, coordinated 360 degree turns in both directions with reversal at various speeds from best glide to min sink.
17. Demonstrates a spiral dive in both directions (not to exceed 60 degrees).
18. Demonstrates one side hill landing.
19. Demonstrates three consecutive landings within 25 feet of a target, safe, smooth on feet and into the wind. Turns are required to set up an approach and avoid overflying the target.
20. Demonstrate proper airspeed for maximum distance flown into a significant headwind (10-15 mph).
21. Demonstrate standard aircraft landing approach: downwind, base, and final when descending through a gradient.
22. Demonstrates proper strong wind landing procedures and how to keep from getting dragged back.
23. Must pass APA Intermediate Written Exam.

Advanced Rating—Required Witnessed Tasks
   The pilot will fly using good judgement and have maturity commensurate with the rating. The following logged requirement must be met:

1. Must have held an Intermediate rating for at least eight months.
2. Must have logged at least 250 flights.
3. Must have logged flights from at least five different sites.
4. Must have logged at least 80 flying days.

5. Must have logged at least 5 flights longer than 30 minutes duration with at least one one-hour flight.
6. Must have logged at least one 30-minute flight in thermal lift without sustaining ridge lift.
7. Must have logged at least 10 flights from a launch at least 2500 ft. above landing zone.
8. Must have flown at least three different types of canopy.
9. 50 hours total air time, with 10 hours in thermal lift.

The following tasks shall be demonstrated:

1. Must show thorough preflight of harness and glider, and a reserve parachute.
2. Verbal analysis of conditions.
3. Flight plan.
4. With each flight, demonstrates method of establishing that pilot is hooked into risers properly prior to launch.
5. Demonstrates proper ground handling of equipment in winds up to 18 mph.
6. All takeoffs should be aggressive, confident and with a smooth transition from running to flying. Flights with slow, unstable launches will not be considered adequate as witnessed tasks.
7. All landings must be safe, smooth, on the feet, and in control.
8. Demonstrates ability to allow clearance when ridge soaring by demonstrating figure eights:
   a) In a wind sufficient to cause drift, two points will be selected on a line perpendicular to the wind. The pilot must fly a figure eight course consisting of smooth turns around the points with the straight segments crossing midway between points.
   b) The pilot must complete two consecutive figure eights around the course compensating for ground track without overcontrol or hesitation.
9. Demonstrates three consecutive spot landings within 10 feet of a target after a flight which requires turns on approach. In smooth conditions, the spot location should be changed by the observer, for each of three flights. Flights should be a minimum of one minute and 300 feet AGL.
10. Demonstrates smooth, coordinated 360 degree turns in both directions with reversal at various speeds from best glide to min sink.
11. Demonstrates a spiral dive in both directions (not to exceed 60 degrees).
12. Demonstrates Ridge Soaring for 15 minutes or more.
13. Demonstrates an altitude gain of at least 500 ft in thermals.
14. At a minimum of 500 feet demonstrates intentional full stalls straight ahead and in turns, showing confident smooth recovery.
15. At a minimum of 500 feet demonstrates front riser canopy collapse and recovery.
16. Demonstrates side hill landings.
17. Successful completion of APA Advanced Written Exam.
18. Must convince the Instructor or Observer that he can check in and fly Advanced rated sites without endangering spectators, other pilots, or jeopardizing the site.

Special Skill Endorsements:
   In order to attain recognition for a special skill, you must follow the requirements listed and perform the skill for observation by an APA Instructor or Observer.

1. Special Skills attainable by Novice and above.
   a) Light Wind Cliff or Ramp Launch:
      1. Demonstrates the ability to launch safely from a shallow slope ramp of cliff top, where running room is severely restricted, drop off is precipitous, wind is 10 mph or less, such that positive attitude control and strong aggressive sprinting starts are required. Stalled, falling/diving launches are not acceptable demonstration even if flight is achieved.
2. Special Skills attainable by Intermediate and above.
   a) Assisted Windy Cliff or Ramp Launch:

1. Demonstrates ability to launch with ground crew assist in windy conditions from precipitous cliff or ramp with strong lift at takeoff. Must show proper use of release signals and confident, controlled, aggressive launch.

b) Turbulence:

1. Demonstrates controlled and unpanicked flight in conditions requiring quick, deliberate substantial and correct control application.

2. Demonstrates controlled and unpanicked recovery from leading edge collapse and over flight.

c) Restricted Landing Field (Spot Landings):

1. Demonstrates a landing using a downwind leg, baseleg and a final leg approach where the entire baseleg, final and landing occur within a 300 foot square.

2. Demonstrates three consecutive landings within 10 feet of a target after a flight which requires turns on approach.

d) Top Landings:

1. Demonstrates three top landings at appropriate site. Must show awareness of rotor conditions with varying wind speeds.

e) Cross Country:

1. Must hold b and c above.

2. Demonstrates ability to recognize a safe landing area from the air and determine and execute a safe approach and landing, accounting for wind direction, rotors, obstacles, power lines, ground slope, vegetation, etc.

3. Must convince Observer or Instructor that he understands the correct use of airspeed to achieve maximum distance over the ground in various conditions of wind, lift, and sink over various types of terrain.

APPENDIX II

RECOMMENDED OPERATING LIMITATIONS

These operating limitations are intended as guidelines to help pilots understand the capabilities of different skill levels. However, these guidelines are only generalities and it should be well understood that every pilot varies in his or her skill and judgement even though they may share the same rating or experience level. Furthermore, each day is different and conditions should be judged on the basis of one's overall experience relating to the wind velocity, gustiness, the temperature, the cloud cover and the terrain.

Our goal is to always fly safely. These guidelines should help you achieve that goal.

Beginner Pilots:
1. Should exceed these limitations only after demonstrating complete mastery of the required Beginner tasks (above), and only after acquiring a full understanding of the potential problems and dangerous situations which may arise from exceeding these limitations.
2. It is highly recommended that all flights be made under the direct supervision of a APA Instructor or Observer.
3. Should fly only in winds of 10 mph or less, with a gust differential of 3 mph.
4. Should launch on slopes of 2:1 to 4:1, where wind is within 15 degrees of being straight up the slope.
5. Should launch only when there are no obstructions within 60 degrees to either side of intended flight path and when pilot may fly straight out from launch to landing with no need to maneuver and no possibility of outflying the landing area.
6. Should maintain flight heading within 15 degrees of directly into the wind.
7. Should fly appropriate sites so as to maintain altitude below 100 AGL.
8. Always wear a helmet and appropriate clothing.

Novice Pilots:
1. Should exceed these limitations only after thoroughly mastering all required tasks after acquiring a full understanding of the potential problems and dangerous situations which may arise from exceeding these limitations.
2. It is highly recommended that all flights be made under the direct supervision of a APA Instructor or Observer.
3. Should fly only in winds of 12 mph or less, with a gust differential of 3-5 mph.
4. Should launch on slopes of 1:1 to 4:1, where wind is within 30 degrees of being straight up the slope.
5. Should launch only when there are few obstructions within intended flight path and there is visual contact with the landing zone.
6. Should maintain heading within 45 degrees of directly into the wind below 300 feet AGL.
7. Try only one new flying skill at a time.
8. Always wear a helmet and appropriate clothing.
9. Flight speed. Should not attempt to fly slowly when encountering lift (minimum sink), but instead concentrate on maintaining best glide, heading, and AIRSPEED. Slow flight must be preceded by stall experience 500' from any object.
10. When learning a new paraglider go to a training site and practice all Beginner and Novice tasks to become familiar with the characteristics of that particular wing.

Intermediate Pilots:
1. Should fly only in winds of 15 mph or less, with a gust differential of 5 mph.
2. Should initiate downwind turns only with 300 feet of clearance outward from the hill or ridge in winds above 15 mph, and 75 feet of clearance in winds above 10 mph.
3. Upon mastering the above skills, an Intermediate pilot should pursue new maneuvers, sites and conditions with the guidance of a APA certified Advanced Instructor or Observer.

4. Always wear a helmet and appropriate clothing.
5. When learning a new paraglider go to a training site and practice all Novice and Intermediate tasks to become familiar with the characteristics of that particular glider.

Advanced Pilots:
1. Should not fly within 50 feet of another glider in smooth air, or 100 feet of another glider in moderately turbulent air.
2. Fly within your skill level for each particular wing that you are flying.
3. Always wear a helmet and appropriate clothing.

APPENDIX III

PARAGLIDING WAIVER

The following document has been designed by lawyers to overcome some of the former problems with waivers. As such it has stood up in court on numerous occasions and is a powerful document for schools and landowners.

Paragliding schools should include the name of their school and the word instructor in the list of activities (first sentence). Pilots wishing to secure flying sites should include the land owner's name in the first parentheses then initial, sign and date the blank areas.

Agreement and Release of Liability

In consideration for being permitted to utilize the facilities or equipment of the (place facility name here) and to engage in the sport of paragliding, solo and two-place flight, and related activities (hereinafter collectively referred to as paragliding hereby agree as follows: I . . . . hereby RELEASE AND DISCHARGE (initial here   ) the (name facility), The American Paragliding Association, any of its members, and any property owners (hereinafter collectively referred to as Released Parties) from any and all liability, claims, demands or causes of action that may hereafter have for injuries and damages arising out of my participation in paragliding activities including but not limited to losses CAUSED BY THE NEGLIGENCE OF THE RELEASED PARTIES (initial here   ). I further agree that I will not sue or make claims against the released parties for damages or other losses sustained as a result of my participation in paragliding activities (initial here   ). I also agree to INDEMNIFY AND HOLD THE RELEASED PARTIES HARMLESS from all claims, judgments and costs, including attorneys fees incurred in connection with any action brought as a result of my participation in paragliding activities (initial here   ). I understand and acknowledge that paragliding activities have inherent dangers that no amount of care, caution, instruction or experience can eliminate and I EXPRESSLY AND VOLUNTARILY ASSUME ALL RISK OF DEATH OR PERSONAL INJURY SUSTAINED WHILE PARTICIPATING IN PARAGLIDING ACTIVITIES WHETHER OR NOT CAUSED BY THE NEGLIGENCE OF THE RELEASED PARTIES (initial here   ). I have been advised and recognize that my paragliding activities are not covered by any personal accident of general liability insurance policy issued to the Released Parties. (initial here   ). I hereby expressly recognize that this Agreement-Release of Liability is contract pursuant to which I have released any and all claims against the Released Parties resulting from my participation in paragliding activities including any claims caused by the negligence of the Released Parties. I hereby confirm that I have been given an option to purchase a waiver of the RELEASE OF LIABILITY CONVENANT NOT TO SUE AND ASSUMPTION OF RISK provisions contained in paragraph 1 and of this agreement at an additional cost of three hundred dollars ($300). I have chosen to (circle and initial one) A. purchase   B. not purchase   this waiver. It is understood that the purchase of the waiver does not constitute contract of insurance but only waiver of the contractual defenses that would otherwise be available to the Released Parties.
I HAVE READ THIS AGREEMENT — RELEASE OF LIABILITY, FULLY UNDERSTAND ITS CONTENTS AND SIGN IT OF MY OWN FREE WILL.

Dated:
Signature:

GLOSSARY

AERODYNAMICS – The study of the movement of a body through the air such as a paraglider wing.

AGL – Abbreviation for Above Ground Level

AIRFOIL – A curved surface designed to generate lift when moving through the air.

AIRSPEED – The velocity of the glider through the air.

AIRSPEED INDICATOR – An instrument for measuring airspeed.

ALTIMETER – An instrument for measuring altitude above a predetermined point.

ATTITUDE – The amount of nose up or nose down in relation to the horizon.

ANGLE OF ATTACK – The angle the relative wind makes with the chord of an airfoil.

APA – American Paragliding Association. The regulatory body for Paragliding in the US.

ASPECT RATIO – Ratio of the span to the chord or $span^2$ divided by surface area.

BANK ANGLE – The angle the wings make with the horizontal in a roll.

BRAKES – The controls of a paraglider that pull down the trailing edge.

CAMBER – The amount of curvature on the upper surface of an airfoil.

CANOPY – The material or "sail" of a paraglider that forms the airfoil or wing.

CELLS – The individual inflated units of a canopy between suspension lines.

CENTER OF GRAVITY – The point along a wing where all the weight is suspended.

CHORD – Measurement of an airfoil from the leading edge to the trailing edge.

COORDINATED TURN – A turn at a steady state in which a slip or a stall does not occur.

CROSS-PORTS – The holes in ribs that allow equalization of pressure between cells.

CROSSWIND – A wind angling across the normal launch or flight path.

CROSS-COUNTRY – Flying beyond the normal landing field by using lift encountered along the way.

DEEP STALL – An emergency situation whereby a glider descends with little or no forward speed.

DOWNWIND – Flying in a direction the same as the wind (flying with a tailwind).

DRAG – The energy losses on the glider due to the friction and mass of the air.

DYNAMIC STALL – A stall produced by pulling the brakes rapidly so that the pilot swings forward and worsens the stall.

END CELL CLOSURE – A problem during inflation whereby the ends of the canopy do not open properly.

FAA – Federal Aviation Administration. The organization that makes the laws regulating paragliding.

FLIGHT CHECK – An inspection after inflation to check for tangled lines or end-cell closures.

GLIDE ANGLE – The angle between the glide path and the horizontal.

GLIDING – Flight that continues from an elevated point to a lower point.

GLIDE PATH – The flight path of a glider.

GLIDER – An aircraft that remains flying through the energy of gravity only.

GLIDE RATIO – The ratio of the distance traveled forward to the distance dropped. This is used interchangeably with L/D.

GORES – The separate panels of a parachute equivalent to cells on a paraglider.

GROUND SPEED – The velocity of a glider over the ground. This is different from airspeed if any wind is present.

GROSS WEIGHT – Total weight of the glider and the heaviest allowed payload (pilot).

HARNESS – A suspension system that supports a pilot and attaches him to a glider.

HEADING – The direction a glider points (this will be different from actual flight direction in a cross wind).

HEADWIND – A wind from the front or opposite the heading.

HORSESHOE STALL – A maneuver whereby full brakes are held until the canopy collapses in the form of a horseshoe.

LEADING EDGE – The forwardmost part of a wing. The spar that forms this forward part.

LIFT – Uprising air used by the pilot to soar.

LIFT TO DRAG RATIO (L/D) – A comparison of the lift forces to the drag forces. See glide ratio.

LOCK-OUT – An out-of-control swinging of the glider to one side with a subsequent nose dive while towing.

LOG BOOK – A book used to list flights and achievements.

MAXIMUM GLIDE RATIO – The best possible glide ratio for a given pilot and glider combination.

MINIMUM SINK RATE – The slowest descent rate possible with a given pilot and glider combination.

MSL – Abbreviation for Mean Sea Level for indicating height above the average sea level.

PITCH – Amount of nose up or nose down. Movement about a lateral axis.

PREFLIGHT CHECK – A careful inspection of the entire flying system before inflation.

RAPID LINK (QUICK LINK) – A small looped device used to attach risers to a harness.

REFLEX – An upward bending of the rear of an airfoil to prevent dives.

RELATIVE WIND – The apparent wind as the glider is flying. Since the glider is always falling in respect to the air around it, the relative wind is different from the actual wind.

RIBS – The vertical panels that separate cells in a canopy.

RISERS – Suspension lines. The lines that attach a harness to the canopy and hold the canopies angle of attack.

ROLL – Lifting or dropping a wing.

ROOT –The center of the wing.

ROTOR – An organized swirl of air behind a cliff face, hill, mountain, building or row of trees.

SINK – Falling air which makes the glider travel downward faster than normal.

SLIP –A falling to the inside of a turn due to insufficient push out.

SOARING – Flight extended beyond the normal glide path of the glider.

SPAN – The total width of a glider from tip to tip.

STABILITY – Tendency for a glider to return to level flight from any attitude or bank.

STABILIZER – A flap or series of cells at the ends of a canopy to help hold it spread.

STALL – A sudden loss of lift and increase in drag due to an excessive angle of attack.

STALLING TURN – A turn with too much inside brake applied resulting in a dropping back of the inside wing followed by a dive.

STEERING LINES – The control or brake lines used to steer a glider or change its speed.

SUSPENSION LINES – Same as risers.

TAILWIND – A wind from the rear or in the direction of heading.

TANDEM – Flying with two persons on one glider.

TELL-TALE – A piece of yarn or cloth on the glider to tell wind direction at takeoff.

THERMAL – A mass of warm rising air providing lift.

THUNDERSTORM – A large convective cell that features violent weather in the form of high winds, turbulence, lightning and hail.

TOGGLES – The hand recepticals or loops at the end of a steering (brake) line.

TOW LINE – The line used to tow gliders with a vehicle.

TRAILING EDGE – The rearward part of a wing.

TURBULENCE – Gusts or swirls of air encountered in flight.

UPWIND – A flight direction heading into the wind.

VARIOMETER – A device that indicates when the glider is rising or sinking.

VELOCITY – A measurement of the speed and direction of motion.

VORTEX (TIP VORTICES) – The swirling of air at the tips of a glider.

WIND GRADIENT – Slowing of the wind as the ground is approached.

WIND SOCK – A cloth tube mounted on a pole to indicate wind direction.

WING LOADING – The weight-to-area ratio on an aircraft found by dividing the flying weight of the pilot plus the glider by the total sail area.

YAW – The motion of a wing whereby one side moves forward and the other moves back.

Index

Notes

Notes